Releasing the Power
ASCEND
of the Human Spirit

Releasing the Power

ASCEND

of the Human Spirit

JAMES L. CATANZARO

CHALICE
PRESS

ST. LOUIS, MISSOURI

Visit Chalice Press on the World Wide Web at
www.chalicepress.com

10 9 8 7 6 5 4 3 2 1   03 04 05 06 07 08

Library of Congress Cataloging–in–Publication Data

Catanzaro, James L.
  Ascend : releasing the power of the human spirit / by James L. Catanzaro.
     p. cm.
  ISBN 0-8272-0051-X (pbk.)
  1. Spiritual life. I. Title.
BL624.C365 2003
204'.4—dc22

2003023520

Printed in the United States of America

Contents

Many seek spiritual power and the life satisfaction they believe it brings, but soon they discover they are not hardwired to spirituality. They desire fulfillment but remain unresolved. They seek happiness but are unclear about where to find it. So they struggle.

Most people report that at critical junctures in life, they are plagued by insecurity, injustice, and insincerity, and they find it difficult to live authentically—consistent with their deeply embedded values and aspirations. These struggles prevent them from achieving and sustaining a sense of spiritual well-being:

1. Insecurity (Feeling Disconnected)
2. Injustice (Being Attacked)
3. Insincerity (Experiencing Betrayal)
4. Inauthenticity (Losing Meaning)

Our research reveals that vital connections—with God, with the sacred, with one's faith tradition, and with others—position searchers to experience spiritual well-being. These connections are made and sealed through commitments:

To Build Authentic Relationships (Trust)
To Respond to the Quiet Voice Within (Belief)
To Listen with the Heart (Empathy)
To Make the Inside Connection (Centered Reflection)

Foreword

Down through the centuries, people of the world have yearned for a more peaceful and harmonious world.

On January 1, 2000, an editorial in *The New York Times* captured the hopes and imaginations of Americans:

> But in these first few hours of a new era, it behooves us to imagine the future with a sense of optimism, something that eluded our ancestors as they struggled just to survive. We have the humane vision and the technological means to lift the world family to new levels of liberty, affluence, health and happiness. Forging that possibility into reality is the task that greets us in the morning of the new millennium.

Dr. James Catanzaro has taken up the challenge. He has gone in search of a way to lift the world to a life "above the struggles." He had a hunch that there is an undiscovered power within individuals that can be tapped for the good of humanity, especially if it is connected with the Spirit of God. In his search, he has talked to literally hundreds of interested people—a purposive sample, not a random sample—of thoughtful people, including people of evident virtue all across the United States, who are searching for the better life: the life above the struggles.

Dr. Catanzaro "listened with his heart" as well as his mind and, after hours of reflection, bit by bit, his thoughts settled into a configuration that gave him the insight of a metaphor that carries the theme of the book: surfing! In essence, this book explains, step by step, how one can be carried forward as on a great wave, experiencing a positive, wonderful feeling that lifts one "above life's struggles." This experience Dr. Catanzaro calls *Scend*. (See his definition on page 9 of the Introduction.) It grants perspective on life, an inspired attitude that turns the struggles into strength-building challenges and raises human beings to a higher level of living.

Is the surfing metaphor real? According to the sample of people Dr. Catanzaro interviewed, there is a phenomenon of "being carried forward as if by a great wave." Seventy-nine percent of Dr. Catanzaro's sample said they knew someone who had been carried forward as if by a great wave. Thirty-four percent said they had personally experienced being carried forward as if by a great wave. Scientists are schooled to be skeptical, but, when a phenomenon occurs, the question is not whether to deny or to believe but rather how to investigate, discover, and explain. The evidence is that Dr. Catanzaro has discovered the phenomenon Scend. He explains to us, step by step, how to achieve Scend and, thereby, spiritual well-being. This book is a manual for spiritual surfing, for being Scent from struggle to spiritual well-being.

This book can lift the world family to new levels, to A-SCEND!

Dr. Donald O. Clifton
Former CEO and Chair of The Gallup Organization

Acknowledgments

This book was enriched greatly by Dr. Don Clifton, whose generous assistance in research design, counsel to present the major theses at the Second Annual Positive Psychology Summit, and ongoing encouragement and positivity proved critical to success. At the outset, Judy Rothman offered valuable assessments of the author's analyses of life struggles and draft chapters. I am indebted to both and thank them for their many expressions of friendship.

Along the way, others helped as well: Rabbi Joseph Klein of Detroit, critiquing the argument of the book; Dennis Weaver, always an inspiration; Dr. Susan Horowitz, offering her experience and insights; Missy Crutchfield, relating to me takes on life in contemporary society; George Gallup, Jr., who has such a remarkable understanding of American spirituality; and Dr. Nell Mohney, who is, above all, my special spiritual role model.

My research was assisted by Anne Bowers Campbell, who also capably prepared the drafts and final manuscript.

Family support, especially that provided by my wife, Rhonda, made the project personally fulfilling and, from the beginning, doable.

A Message from the Author

Most of us, at some point in life, struggle. It's a nearly universal experience. When we ask those in struggle "Why?" more times than not, the answer comes down to finding meaning and purpose in life. We want happy marriages and rewarding careers; most important, we desire spiritual well-being. But that is easier said than done.

I've been engaged in a spiritual search for most of my adult years. It's a journey more and more of us are taking. The new century may well be dominated by the discovery of inner space, as the last was of outer space.

My search has taken me nearly a lifetime—with bumps and bruises along the way—to claim the power of transformation, the elevating and sustaining presence of God. I want to share with you how the experience of happiness can be enhanced, faith strengthened, and life above "The Struggles" established; how well-being rooted in authenticity, inner connectedness, openness to the sacred, and union with God can be enjoyed every day.

I have been helping people rise above spiritual struggle for several decades—as a minister and educator, first in Southern California, then in the Midwest, and, presently, in the South. I have a feel for how people throughout the country view the challenges to spiritual living, and I've seen *Scend*—the spiritual dimension recognized and developed in this book—transform lives!

Undergirding this work are many sources: an extensive study of the spiritual lives of Americans conducted in consultation with Dr. Donald Clifton, longtime leader of The Gallup Organization; many insights gained from focus groups; dialogue with leading commentators on contemporary life; hard lessons; magical experiences; and deep convictions. These have enabled me to map spiritual struggle, and they have exposed and confirmed Scend—the affirming spirit within us—as the key to living past "The Struggles" and achieving sustained spiritual well-being.

What are "The Struggles"? They boil down to this: knowing there is much more to life than experienced, but feeling held back from achieving the happiness, the security, the well-being sought so passionately. We know life can't be "picture perfect," but, sometimes, we find ourselves constrained from within. We just can't keep purpose and meaning as everyday companions. Other times, we feel assaulted—by destructive events in our lives, by the corrosive effects of social change, by the contagion of insecurity. When our struggles get the best of us, they keep us from the positive outlook and personal fortitude needed to propel us forward to ongoing spiritual well-being.

Fortunately we *are* connected. This is the message of the book. We can, therefore, a-Scend above spiritual struggle. This book is about using our fundamental connections to bring us to tranScendent living.

The perspective of this book is undeniably Christian. Nevertheless, it is written to strengthen the journey for all who seek spiritual well-being—happiness and contentment founded upon affirming relationships with God, with other children of God, and with one's own essential self.

It's a transformed life we seek, one that taps continuously into the reservoir of strength within—our authentic self in communion with God, a life where peak experiences define our common experience, and openness, trust, forgiveness, and love are ever-expanding.

> Don't struggle over anything; but in all things—through prayer and supplication coupled with thanksgiving—make your requests known to God. And the peace of God that is beyond all understanding will guard your hearts and minds through Christ Jesus. (Phil. 4:6–7)

Introduction

*M*any seek spiritual power and the life satisfaction they
believe it brings, but soon they discover they are not
hardwired to spirituality. They desire fulfillment but remain
unresolved. They seek happiness but are unclear about where
to find it. So they struggle.

Spirituality[1] is a relatively new term in the discourse of
religion in the West. It has been a centerpiece for New Age
writers and followers, and it has made its way into everyday
twenty-first-century language. Its origins may be more Eastern
than Western. Nevertheless, it describes a state many Americans
of all persuasions say they want to achieve.

Most people report that they are unclear about the precise
meaning of *spirituality*. Based on interviews with leading clerics
and religious scholars from every major world religion, who,
themselves, are not always certain about what the word conveys,
the following working definition will be used throughout the
book: "a state of transparent well-being produced by
transforming relationships"—with one's "self,"[2] important
others, the sacred, the Transcendent (God).

How do these relationships come about? I once was
sure they came from right belief, right conduct, and right

1

worship. Early in my search for spiritual well-being, I had two life-transforming epiphanies that forever changed that view. The dean of my college—Dean Terrell B. Crum, a man of modest income, exceptional intellectual attainment, and transparent spiritual depth; an orthodox Christian by anyone's definition—took me as his "mentee" one winter night to a downtown church in Boston where he was to preach.

After an inspiring service, he surprised everyone present when he bolted past the faithful toward the rear of the sanctuary and then turned—as if possessed—to make his way to a vagrant huddled in back. Without a moment's hesitation, he took his new overcoat and draped it around him. I was amazed—and warmed!

It was, for me, powerful, life-defining—a special revelation!—and not just because of the impact of sacrificial acts of kindness or of the extraordinary goodness of this man. It was an experience of feeling the presence of a great, enabling, inspiring force that had moved him—from his innermost self—to remarkable empathy, care, and generosity; and me to reflection on my own spiritual capacity. Compressed into thirty seconds was, I felt certain, the essence of spiritual well-being. On reflection, I realized the dean had displayed, with extraordinary transforming power, oneness with God, God's people, and his essential self.

Several years later, I found myself the student of a renowned theologian, John B. Cobb, Jr., who in so many ways works outside the fold of orthodox Christianity. I was astonished that he, too, exhibited the same compelling, primal force, in virtually every encounter I had with him. He is a model of spirituality.

These experiences turned out to be more transforming than years of theological study. They brought me to see that when the human spirit is elevated through graced relationships, it transforms lives—ours, and those about us. The human spirit is, indeed, the lamp of God (Prov. 20:27).

What is so special about this insight? *Whatever our faith tradition or our spiritual standing*, we are schooled to believe spirituality comes from confessing our weaknesses, then looking *outside*[3] for help, rather than celebrating our strengths and releasing the positive power within. Our research into spirituality reveals that most people have witnessed, at least once, the inspiring power of God's spirit in others, but only a few say they experience that power within themselves.[4] It also reveals that most believe, unfortunately, that this power cannot be fully theirs.

Years later, I had two further epiphanies. Exhausted from an all-night flight to England but wishing to be friendly, I offered a meager greeting to the woman behind the hotel check-in counter: "How are you doing?"

"*Struggling through*," she replied.

Somewhat surprised, I countered: "Why would you answer that way?"

"That's what we Londoners often say when you ask that question."

"Tell me why," I continued my inquiry.

"Well, that's what life is, isn't it? A struggle? At least, here."

Perhaps it is, I thought, No, surely, it is!

After a few days in London, I began to see her point. Of course, American life is no less helter-skelter. We, too, struggle—at times, down to our last emotion—though we typically respond in a more affirmative manner: "Fine," "Good enough," "OK."

A few months after my London trip, I visited New York City. This time, it was the woman behind the hotel check-in counter who asked *me*, "How are you today?"

"Struggling through," I said, attempting to gain a revealing response.

I did. "You'll find a number of churches nearby; we're known for our churches," she insisted. Obviously, she assumed I had spiritual problems, probably because our struggles in America, like those of the British, so often resolve down to our ongoing search for life's purpose, for what connects us to our innermost selves, to what is transcendent—ultimately, to what will enable us to overcome life's struggles. More than 75 percent of those we surveyed report that they are not satisfied with their spiritual life—that they struggle. Our studies also uncovered that spiritual well-being and struggle are, in many ways, polar opposites.[5] So we learned: Overcome "The Struggles" and you will take a first step toward spiritual well-being. Build essential connections and you will achieve and sustain spiritual well-being.[6]

1. "The Struggles," Happiness, and Spirituality

Pushing past struggle is not accomplished easily. The fact is, whether we are mildly happy, pretty happy, very happy, or unhappy, most of us struggle—especially for spiritual well-being. During the past twenty years, research psychologists have uncovered that most Americans—and Europeans—say that they are happy (more than 80 percent, in fact).[7] Yet many report, at the same time, they experience troubling setbacks with intimate partners, in their careers, and, most profoundly, in their relationship with God—in fact, just as many who claim to be happy reported this as did those who see themselves as unhappy![8]

It turns out that a positive disposition doesn't connect us to our inner selves or to the Transcendent, and it doesn't steel us against life struggles. It improves sociability, perhaps career success, maybe even longevity,[9] but it isn't an elixir for overcoming struggle. We just can't smile away deeply rooted feelings of insecurity, isolation, emptiness, or exposure to injustice—especially undeserved and unforeseen acts of violence (by humans as well as nature).

So, whether people accept the comments of these hotel clerks or the findings of social psychologists, whether they are English or American, their everyday experience is not idyllic, healing, and transforming.

No, more times than not, the daily routine is "struggling through"—slugging it out!

There's no surprise here. Life is complex,[10] often stressful, and frighteningly at risk since September 11, 2001, with random acts of violence and nuclear proliferation rampant. In any case, change is, so many times, discontinuous; rather than evolutionary, slow, and predictable, it's revolutionary, rapid, and unexpected. It comes so abruptly, it's often "in your face." Just a moment's reflection on the stock market or the impact of new technologies on our lives makes this point clear.

As far as everyday relationships are concerned, they usually have to be negotiated and then renegotiated. And there are no magic pills or quick fixes when we run into trouble—despite therapists, mood elevators, spiritual gurus, and a spate of self-help books that may deliver brief happiness spikes but virtually always drop us back into the doldrums. And in our religious lives, we often experience the same roller-coaster ride. We look to *outside* powers, to external authorities to raise our spirits, to carry us through, but looking *outside* doesn't take us to ongoing security or to the spiritual well-being we seek. Instead, as we will learn, getting a hold on struggle and attaining spirituality come from making an *inside* connection, marrying aspiration to inspiration. This is the view of many theologians I have interviewed and of average citizens in our sample, though both are unclear how this might occur.

Nevertheless, they generally agree: Spirituality[11] is expressed in moral bearing, celebration of the ennobling, care for others, in devotional, sacramental life—above all, in resilience in the face of destructive struggle.

Often spirituality takes form through religious commitment. Sometimes it takes other forms. Religion usually derives from personal history, lineage, family, ethnicity, culture, station in life.[12] Spirituality, on the other hand, transcends religious traditions and speaks of personal experience of what is of "ultimate concern."[13] Nine out of ten of our survey respondents agreed that they have a spiritual dimension, but only one-quarter believe they approach spiritual satisfaction in life. They struggle.

So to sum it up, our research shows spiritual well-being is attained by transforming defeating struggles into strength-building challenge, and by reorienting thinking and living past being religious (bound to a tradition) to being *internally* driven (inspired) to empowered living where—each day—we are carried forward by a wave of positivity, the power of God.

2. Life above "The Struggles"

Nearly twenty-five hundred years ago, the philosopher Aristotle ventured that the highest of all goods is happiness. But he was quick to offer that we all differ about what happiness is.[14] Ever since, great minds around the world have labored to prove him wrong, to describe the ultimate happiness.

But the nature of human happiness is still debated. For most definitions of happiness, two components are key—not letting life's struggles weigh us down, and feeling spiritually whole.[15] People commonly describe happiness as they do spiritual well-being: living from resilience, out of inner resourcefulness; turning struggles from downers to encouragers, from debilitating to rehabilitating.

One way to picture the happiness that comes from spiritual well-being is to imagine a forward-leaning action figure in motion. The figure is of a person making evident progress, building on strengths and establishing vital connections. A closer look reveals that this figure's forward movement is by inner propulsion. No one or thing is pushing. The final, face-to-face shot signals that this person is energized by transforming power, turning conflict into stimulating give-and-take, setbacks into cushioned falls, and struggle into invigorating challenge. The countenance is warm and expressive, truly human.[16] This action figure is taking it to life rather than being taken on by life's ups and downs. Life has an upward trend line. Contrary to John Cougar Mellencamp, life goes on *and* the thrill of living stays on.

Even the spiritually adept are quick to concede, however, that spiritual well-being is not nirvana: continuous peace, tranquility, and victory. We all run into resistance, stumble, feel tedium in life. We all encounter great forces arrayed against us—our genetic makeup, timing, fate, aging. And we all recognize that whatever our background, gender, status in life, or most recent birthday, struggles can corner us and take the joy out of life, and they can take the life out of moments of joy. The good news is that these struggles need not shatter hopes and carry us to "the blues." In a new century filled with hope, yet pregnant with uncertainty, even uncontrolled mortal threat, we need not answer "How are you doing?" with *"Struggling through."* We can live without being held captive by fear and struggle; we can see the glass as half full; we can be empowered; we can be resilient and resourceful.

Perhaps for the first time in human history—given extended life, burgeoning wealth, work without great ardor and pain, time to "smell the roses," instant communication to alert us to danger and tell us of opportunity—despite all the threats, many feel they can achieve a heightened quality of life, even happiness, even spiritual well-being.[17] But can they *sustain* well-being? Can they live above struggle? After all, struggle seems to be part of the human condition. It's making concerted, sometimes agonizing efforts to gain life satisfaction but feeling held back by adversity, vicarious bad events, addictions, other people's expectations, past decisions, low aspirations, concern about our weaknesses, and—most consequentially—frayed relationships. Being caught in the middle—feeling vulnerable but yearning for security, having inner doubt but desiring confidence, knowing setbacks but seeking God's strength—*that* is struggle. We struggle when we seek more out of life but can't break the constraints that prevent us from experiencing every day a powerful sense of well-being, when we strive to do something we know to be most difficult of all—*to live empowered, fulfilled, connected, resolved, and inspired.*

Most people we surveyed believe they are on the road to overcoming struggle, but they confess it is difficult to make spiritual well-being their everyday companion. They *know* what spiritual well-being is but they are not certain they can attain it: life as a rush, feeling on top even when we're not necessarily on top, carried forward, undergirded by an optimistic and enthusiastic outlook, working from strengths,[18] readied to withstand life's attacks, encouraged to live through purpose and with meaning, feeling the hand of God every day in our lives.

Being spiritually whole means being satisfied with who we are, where we are right now, and where we are going— even if we are not the heroic characters of our adolescent dreams, leading or saving the world. Being spiritually whole means feeling inspired—carried forward as if by a mighty wave, as if by Scend. Our research shows this insight to be quintessential to understanding spirituality.

3. The Power of Scend

What is Scend?[19] In its Old English origins, it's a nautical term that refers to the driving force of the sea, of the spurt forward of a vessel being carried along by a great swell.

As a lifelong body surfer, I understand the Scend of the sea. I know the liberating whoosh, the true exhilaration of being propelled beachward by an angry wave—to the serenity of foam and sand. It's psychologically—every bit as physically— renewing. It is a Scend! *And* I know how difficult it is to get into position to capture a wave, how every wave in the sea brings *new* challenge. *But* I am confident, as well, that each wave offers wondrously new possibilities.

I've experienced Scend also in human relations. It's bonding with another, soul to soul. It's "chemistry" bringing new life to relationships. I recall the end of a euphoric day of surfing great waves and enjoying with my wife the comfort of being alone on the magnificent Crane's Beach of Barbados. We picked up our belongings and began our trek to our car nearly a quarter-mile away.

Suddenly, from out of the junglelike brush that bordered the beach, a young Bajan man came running. Wonderfully, realizing his appearance could be interpreted as threatening, he slowed down, threw up his hands, and shouted, "Don't worry, I'm not an American." We were relieved!

We welcomed his arrival; his exclamation, however, sent us to ponder for weeks to come about what kind of a culture and image we Americans have created.

But our unexpected embrace of words and arms that day with our stranger-friend brought to both of us a sense of the human spirit we share. We felt carried forward by a warm and healing impulse—Scend—connecting us cityfolk and a man of the islands.

Spiritual Scend *is the power of the spirit—God's spirit—expressed in our lives as a surge of positivity and optimism, as redemptive, as transforming, like a mighty wave. It's being inspired, seeking out and embracing people, and, most important, knowing we can overcome any obstacle through inner strength because it's God's strength.*

The Scend experience often comes in a flash, unexpectedly and at momentous times—when people are in crisis, when they experience triumph, when they connect "soul to soul" with others—for many, when they encounter Jesus as the Christ. Sometimes, Scend is experienced in the calm of gardening or walking in the rain. Scend encounters take us to our roots, to deeply embedded values and aspirations, to inner warmth and resolution. Most important, they unite us with others in a common bond, and they color our life "happy." Can Scend be an everyday partner?

Researchers tell us that those who win big lottery jackpots stay euphoric only for a short time.[20] Their new financial standing replaces the old but, as before, it's insufficient. Expectations have risen even beyond their new means. And, soon, there are complications: family and friends—close and remote—want a share in their new wealth; more possibilities pull at the winners; and, in a short time, they aren't clear whether people are with them because they like them or because they want to exploit them. Material pleasure, in any case, is transitory.

I was sitting on the curb outside a convenience store, enjoying a double-dip ice-cream cone with my four-year-old grandson, Trey. "What makes you happy?" I asked him.

"Eating chocolate ice cream," he replied quickly.

A few minutes later came an unexpected request: "Can I throw my cone in the trash?" He still had a scoop to go, but I nodded approval.

Then I commented: "I thought you said eating chocolate ice cream makes you happy."

He paused and observed insightfully, "Yes, but not now."

It is well established that sustained happiness is not directly a product of affluence,[21] nor is it derived from sex, power, position, or drugs. Happiness is lasting when it comes from tapping the affirming and elevating power *within* us and in life, the power of God. Living empowered by Scend releases us from destructive effects of struggle. Bad events in life (we can't always dodge or discount them) do not hold us down when we are resolved—self-assured and satisfied with life—whatever fate throws against us. The people we studied who report they have attained high spirituality say typically: "When the Spirit guides us, we grow *through* our struggles and experience an ever-expanding sense of well-being, of spiritual peace." It's like that lighthearted lilt we feel when we have won something big or gone to the beach on an early summer day.

4. The Formula

Are there actions people take that translate into Scend-filled living? Our research points to three:

- Doing the disciplined work of getting into position—getting control of spiritual struggle;
- Launching ourselves forward through loyalty, belief, empathy, and connection; then, finally,
- Letting go, so we are carried forward by a great force—in, around, under, and through us.

Again, my thoughts are drawn inexorably to *surfing:* riding a giant, exploding mountain of water down the chute into the froth of sand and sea. It's a totally exhilarating experience—in today's language: awesome. You work yourself through the turbulence into the swell until you're in position, ready for launch. When your vault forward is attuned to the wave's releasing power, you are transformed into a quiet-yet-powerful missile. Then, you glide harmlessly into the calm and sink into head-to-toe relaxation.

Yes, you're bruised and jostled here and there. Small protrusions poke you, sand and shells scrape at your body, the jarring power of the water alarms you, but the overall experience is—in reality—breathtaking. It's a Scend! The cool water kisses your face, your heart jumps with joy and you exclaim, "More! More!"

That feeling is akin to the contentment with life our research sample say they desire in life—an afterglow—not just in extraordinary moments (as about half of those we queried report they have experienced), but daily undergirding every moment (only six percent say they share this lifestyle). It's *life above destructive struggles.* It doesn't come naturally, especially as we are programmed by modern society. So, as we wander life's beaches, we have to look for "perfect" waves, position ourselves right and, once *set*, take courage, and *go!*

This book explores spiritual surfing, breaking clear from thrashing about in the waters of life to being propelled forward through transforming connections as if by a great swell—Scend. It's about getting above the core struggle that unsettles our relationships at home, at work, in life—about our struggle to find spiritual wholeness: purpose, meaning, transcendence, fulfillment. It's about positioning ourselves to be carried forward to remarkable kindness, quiet strength, and enduring satisfaction, so the power of God's spirit resident within us can be released into our lives and the lives of others around us.

5. The Commitments

Historically, followers of most religions, particularly those from the Near East (Judaism, Christianity, and Islam) look to the god above the world to get them past troubles, to provide sanctuary against the forces that overrun them as individuals.[22]

People want struggles with partners and coworkers—as well as with body image, weight, addictions, personal finance, health, troublesome neighbors, business competitors, and the like—to be quieted and resolved…supernaturally! Just listen to their prayer requests. But, so many times, despite prayer and petition, these struggles run their course. *Outside* help only arrives occasionally, and more likely than not simply by good fortune. Fervent prayer, and ardent religious commitment, in other words, do not predictably produce these desired outcomes. Fate usually wins out.

To live above the threats and vicissitudes of life requires that we are open to self[23] *and to God's voice within.* Then, we can take on life each day with confidence and from strength, and we can handle whatever comes at us from over the horizon.

There may well be a number of ways to promote Scend-filled living. Our study through focus groups and survey science reveals that making five specific life commitments and recording them in our spiritual muscle memories invariably produces a state of transparent well-being—spirituality.

These commitments build one upon the other, from the easiest to make to the most difficult, from what is foundational to spiritual well-being to what delivers us there. Our study shows they work in lives from coast to coast, whatever one's gender or station in life. They bring people into the releasing power of spiritual waves—to life through Scend.

6. The Approach

Although only 25 percent of adult Americans say they are satisfied spiritually, more than 80 percent of those questioned recount that they have encountered others who are "inspired" and "spiritually satisfied." Apparently, most know paragons of spirituality—saints—but few have found the pathway to spiritual living. The extraordinary success of the Holiness Movement worldwide shows how widespread and magnetic is this interest. As a rule, people even into the twenty-first century still want to increase their spiritual standing. They want to imitate Christ. They want to work out their own salvation, though not necessarily in fear and trembling.

This book recounts how scholars and everyday seekers have found spiritual well-being. Each chapter contains stories that illustrate real-life struggles and proven steps to freedom from their numbing effects. Some stories have been merged with others to protect the privacy of those involved; others are just as they occurred. Story sharing is a powerful way to communicate and elevate spiritual standing. It is the approach most scholars believe early Christian writers took as they framed the gospel. It clearly is the way ancient Jewish writers told of their God and their role in his world. So our search for spirituality takes us from being overwhelmed by the waves of life to riding them to safety, authenticity, and the truly good and virtuous life.

7. The Assumptions

The overriding assumptions of this book are that we can learn about and achieve spiritual well-being as people tell of their journeys in pursuit of spirituality, that everyday people can release the power of the spirit (God's spirit) within, that when they do, their lives are transformed positively, and that when it's said and done, most of us want to release that power.

I

Understanding "The Struggles"

M̲ost people report that at critical junctures in life, they
are plagued by insecurity, injustice, and insincerity,
and they find it difficult to live authentically—consistent with
their deeply embedded values and aspirations. These struggles
prevent them from achieving and sustaining a sense of spiritual
well-being.

Americans are experiencing a dramatic upsurge in interest
in things spiritual, especially since September 11, 2001. Four
of five say they want to grow spiritually,[1] to feel connected
essentially and positively with their inner selves, important
others, the sacred, and, most of all, with what is "Greater"—
God. Most desire to live out their inner longings and deeply
embedded values, to have meaning, purpose, authenticity—to
be spiritually based. They want their relationships to be fulfilling
and enduring. They want personal security and the feeling
that they can make the world a fair and safe place in which to
operate. They want their spiritual journey to be a wellspring

of happiness. For those who are Christian, they want to experience every day the healing spirit of Christ: truly loving God, their very selves, and others about them—and feeling the warmth of their love in return.

Even those who say their spiritual lives are strong, however, when asked at given times about their present sense of spiritual well-being, confess they have doubts that pull them into struggle—away from spiritual well-being. Doubts can lead to spiritual bankruptcy—death by a thousand fears. When people fear their spiritual search will fall short, they falter. And, when this unsettled outlook has "high power" (when skepticism and negativity make sense of a great deal of the world) and when it is easy to confirm (bad things are happening—all the time!), a turnaround can't be made readily.[2] Spiritual struggle ensues, and it is difficult to shake.

So people nationwide—in cities large and small, suburbs, rural areas, even idyllic outposts—commonly report they experience life as though they are swimming in dangerous waters. Life, for them, is struggle; spiritual well-being—life above destructive struggle—though highly sought after, remains elusive.

As it turns out, the spiritual search is like the quest for the perfect holiday. Usually it doesn't turn out the way the travel agent promised.

I was vacationing in Cancun several winters ago following the lure of warmth and adventure. One morning I set out for Isla Mujeres, a small island off the coast—a skin diver's paradise.

I prepared carefully for the boat ride and the day— wearing just a swimsuit, an old T-shirt and thongs, with mask and fins in hand and with a U.S. twenty-dollar bill and some pesos in my back pocket.

Once on the island, while strolling down the beach, I spied a massive formation jutting out of the water about a hundred yards offshore—an entrancing spot for lunch, I thought. So I bought a sandwich with my pesos, left behind my thongs and shirt, and began my swim to serenity, sandwich arm held high. My plan seemed perfect, but life rarely is that way. What happened next was wild and woolly.

As I tired, my "sandwich hand"—without my realizing it—dropped beneath the surface of the water and set off total pandemonium below. Fish of all sizes ascended on me in a virtual feeding frenzy—devouring the food, biting my hand, and sending me into such convulsions that my twenty-dollar bill came loose from my pocket and was torn to pieces as it floated to the surface.

I was in strange waters—as it turned out, perilous ones at that! My well-laid plans didn't take into account the real dangers before me, but, by the best of fortune, my day was saved by honeymooners from Houston who loaned me money for food and the boat ride back.

Most people experience life this way—they begin with high hopes and grand plans, and they have some initial success. There is the exhilaration of adventure. But, partway to the destination, they run into "spoilers" that interrupt their plans and strip them of security. Sometimes, luck is on their side and they are rescued; other times, though perhaps only momentarily, they are sent into convulsive struggle. Why doesn't God bail them out? Why are they put to the test?

When we asked a cross section of people (including devout churchgoers) whether on random occasions they felt—*in that moment*—spiritually whole, connected with God, secure, more than two-thirds said, "No." Not surprising! *Most faiths recognize that the struggle for spiritual wholeness requires ongoing renewal, continuous touchpoints* to keep followers on course, special ceremonies and retreats to light anew spiritual flames. Yes, we believe; no, we aren't always spiritually empowered. We struggle. And since spiritual struggle, by definition, arises from the core of one's being, it can be truly daunting. For most of my adult years, I have labored to get past it.

My seminary training, doctorate in philosophy of religion, and ministerial experience didn't hardwire me, as I expected, to spiritual satisfaction. On the contrary, the spiritual pursuit turned out to be complicated, not simplified, by study and intellectual assent. Study and assent, most times, take seekers to the brain instead of to faith, and, as is said in popular lore, it's a long trip from the mind to the heart. Study and assent also put people in tension with their other beliefs, and, sometimes, even require them to distort or deny universally accepted understandings of the world. Study also may bring into focus perplexing conflicts within the scriptures, in theology, in faith, in living. In any case, almost always, the search for truth is focused on traditions—the past—not on personal daily problems and finding effective solutions. *As a result, spirituality and religiosity don't always come together. Indeed, sometimes, they are contraries!*

Religion, especially in the Western world, traditionally reduces spiritual struggle to the workings of others, even evil powers. The promise of relief, therefore, rests with an *intervening* God. This is the strength of these traditions, and it is their profound weakness. So, customarily, there are moments of elation as the faithful celebrate "answers to prayers." But, then, there are moments of confusion and disappointment when God does not respond. The good die from pancreatic cancer in the same percentages and with the same anguish as the bad (though, in general, the righteous do live longer because of their own efforts).[3] Notre Dame and Liberty University football teams win and lose with a frequency that seems entirely unrelated to the fervor of the prayers in the locker room before the game.[4]

And here's another dilemma: Religious traditions often steer the faithful into conflict with those holding other points of view—scientific, secular, humanistic, to name a few, to say nothing of those representing other religious doctrines and expressions. Because spirituality builds on openness to others, preoccupation with doctrines that define who is "in" and who is "out" actually takes seekers away from the spiritual life, not to it. This is the reason why ideology and dogma so commonly yield judgment, vilification, even violence—not Christlike care for others. The long and tortured histories of Judaism, Christianity, and Islam make this point with exclamation.

So, here is the predicament: The faithful labor to understand, but their study may confound them as well as bring them into tension with the followers of alternative persuasions. They believe, but their beliefs don't always speak to their struggles or enable them to find a way out through a vision of a hopeful future that is within their control.[5] Too often, they drive through life glued to their rearview mirrors, unable to relate affirmatively with the new diversity about them.

It is recognized universally that "believers" are not notably freer than others from insincerity, insecurity, inner doubt, insensitivity, pettiness, misconduct, rumormongering, and materialism. They do not live remarkably above the injustices of the world. Many times, it is they who perpetuate them! Put more kindly: We all are flawed, at times quite frail; and we all are vulnerable to random violence, disease, and misfortune. And so, spiritual struggle is pervasive!

Despite inconsistent conduct and a welter of belief, *most agree on the indicators of spiritual well-being:* My focus group participants generally concurred—spiritual persons live a life that is

- consistent with their beliefs and ideals
- close to God and the sacred
- free of insincerity
- connected with others through forgiveness and compassion
- propelled by essential goodness and soaring by virtue of their strengths

So this is the challenge: People have a pretty fair idea of what spiritual well-being looks like, but this knowledge doesn't necessarily translate into escape from spiritual struggle.

Why are so many caught up in spiritual struggle? Most often, the reason is negative orientation.[6] Our research shows that negativity pulls people into four engrossing struggles: with insecurity, with injustice, with insincerity, and with inauthenticity.

1. The Struggle with Insecurity

I was shocked by my mother's panic when she was to have a hysterectomy. By everyone's account, she was a saint—a respected Bible teacher, a moral giant, a model of Christian living. My shock came from her response to going under the knife for a significant, but not mortally threatening, procedure. It spoke of a deep insecurity, one I didn't expect from a person who traveled each moment with God. I hadn't realized she lived in profound spiritual struggle. As I discovered, as strong as her faith was, it couldn't carry her through this life event with assurance of recovery. She believed she was in the hands of an all-powerful and loving God who knew her as his special child; nevertheless, she wasn't confident of the outcome.

My mother is not unique. It's common for people to report that they yearn to be close to God, to be at peace—above all, to have inner confidence—but nevertheless to fall short. Most people speak of uncertainty about what is to be their life course and, in crisis moments, invariably fall prey to the paralyzing force of insecurity.

We assure ourselves God will sustain us in our hour of need but we are—still—fraught with apprehension. Will God be there for us? Will he rescue us? I recall the words of desperation of New York City firefighter Anthony Pasquali the day the World Trade Center towers fell to rubble. A CNN reporter asked about his buddies, most likely caught in the catastrophe. "Hopefully," he sighed, "God is with us." We now know: God did not rescue them!

Of course, most people don't awaken every day shackled by anxiety and spiritual insecurity. And there are times their struggles yield positive results. They may even drive them to peak performance. But, with uncommon exception, prolonged spiritual struggle does debilitate. Yes, we have luminous times. We feel God is with us; things are going right; we feel strong, confident, empowered. But these occasions are—more often than not—fleeting, especially when crisis comes and threats to our well-being from financial misfortune to disease to terrorism loom. So, most seekers' lives are punctuated by ups and downs. They hope to be embraced by God, but they stumble and lose their way; they feel connected, then disconnected, at risk—in a word, insecure. This is why, when people in my focus groups are asked to describe their spiritual struggles, invariably they begin with something like this: "Sometimes, God answers, and sometimes, for reasons I guess known by God alone, God is silent."

Why do these normal-as-blueberry-pie outbreaks of insecurity keep us from spiritual well-being? I gained a new perspective on anxiety over several clear winter nights in Utah. Some of our anxieties stem from events in our lives years ago.

Every evening for a week, two weary skiers shared with me our resort spa. We related stories of our escapades on the slopes and occasional insights into our everyday lives back home. The second night, we were joined by Margot. She was a nonskier who had come to the mountains to escort her teenage son and daughter. By the end of her second sojourn with us, she had changed the focus of our conversations. Margot was in spiritual crisis and she wanted help—from us, safe strangers far from her home locale.

A minister's wife, she felt she had to be a model of spirituality, at least around her husband's parishioners. "I'm called on to counsel women in crisis, young people trying to sort out relationship and sexual issues," she confided, "but I'm not the person they think I am." We spoke that evening of the painful difficulty of living up to the unrealistic expectations of others.

The next evening, when Margot took her place in the spa, our discussion quickly moved off ski runs and nettlesome snowboarders back to her plight. This time, she took us from the struggle of living a sainted life to how base insecurities keep us from spiritual peace.

"Whatever the scriptures say," she confided to me, "I don't believe I'm forgiven."

"What is it," I asked quietly, "that has so shaken your confidence?"

After a moment of tortured silence, she whispered to me, "When I was twenty, I had an affair with my pastor and had to have an abortion to protect our reputations." She was overcome by grief, though she tried to regain her composure by apologizing for revealing these "terrible things."

I felt compelled to embrace her with words of comfort and understanding. It was her last night on the mountain.

Margot sent a note to me a few weeks later. She felt "a giant weight" had been lifted off of her. She was going to keep her secret in her heart, but her counseling ministry now will reflect more forgiveness.

Most people do not experience the depth of Margot's anxieties, but they may carry around burdens from past personal episodes that fuel insecurity. Simply living in America since the terrorist strikes of September 2001 and recalling the calamity of the day are sufficient reasons to feel vulnerable and burdened. The words of reporters and witnesses seemed inadequate vessels to contain and carry the shock, the horror of that day—and many that followed. September 11—at the very least—punctured our canopy of well-being.

So, there are times when we feel elated, exuberant, strong, and with a sense that anything is possible, but there are other times when we are threatened, unsure about our future, when we say with Lawrence Ferlinghetti, "The world is a beautiful place to be born into, if you don't mind a touch of hell now and then."[7]

Insecurity is a key roadblock to sustained spiritual well-being.

2. The Struggle with Injustice

I stopped by Aunt Martha's Pancake House in Chicago one morning on my way to work. Sitting in a nearby booth was a man who fixed on me with a glaring stare. Finally, he got up and stood over me—menacingly. "Can I help you?" I attempted to get him to back off and reveal his problem.

"My cousin used to clean doormats for your college," he barked. "You cut him out. Now, he's hurtin'. If I have my way, you'll hurt too."

I was president of the college, but I knew nothing about his cousin's plight. Fortunately, this man never came into my view again, but, that day, he brought me great discomfort.

We all are subject to unprovoked, even unreasoned assaults. Virtually all of us are subject, as well, to the greater injustice of having aches and pains brought on by the "countless imperfections of our bodies...revealed by the passage of time."[8] Many suffer due entirely to unfortunate genetics.

These kinds of "injustices"—random events and built-in failures—bring us to the near-universal recognition: *The things we most care for too many times are at the mercy of things we care for the least.* We care for personal and family financial security, so we invest. And we care little for those who act selfishly and dishonestly. But, as in Enron, they may mismanage the companies in which we place our life savings and create havoc in our lives by their perfidious deeds. We strive to find a "just" existence, but we are reminded—time and again—that we live in a world often void of fairness, no matter how hard we strive to make it right. So we struggle.

Rita's bout with injustice came from her workplace affiliations. As spokesperson for her faculty union local, she stepped into a line of fire she found outrageously unfair.

Rita joined our focus group of high school faculty and staff one afternoon. She was seething with anger, overcome with hurt. She had been singled out at the previous night's school board meeting by the governing body's chairman for being "more concerned for the advancement of your teacher union than for your students." She was livid and recoiling.

With a reputation as an outstanding teacher and with a string of stellar evaluations in her file, she was justifiably angry. "Our world here is monstrously unfair," she erupted. "Little people, like this clueless chairman, want to crush our spirits."

She wasn't alone in her feelings. The entire group was dispirited. The chairman's statements had reminded them ruefully that they don't always operate in a just world. When they pressed for salary improvement, they incurred the overreaching wrath of the school board.

It was for Rita and the others present an agonizing time. A person who should have bargained with her respectfully and confidentially had humiliated her before her very peers.

Our session focused on the real architecture of life, on how our lives often are interrupted rudely by those who want us to be and do like someone else, how these ugly interruptions drain spiritual strength out of us and leave us in despair.

We live every day with injustices—the exploitative attacks of others upon us (like those of the school board chairman on Rita), the unfair judgments people make of us (like the menacing assertions I heard from a stranger on an otherwise fine day), and the unexpected and unwarranted perils of disease, accident, frailty, natural disaster, violence, and terrorism. It's difficult to cope with these injustices because they visit us, most times, unexpectedly—sometimes with cruel force. They have the power, at any moment, to shatter our hopes and dreams. We try to live free of them; we expect God to shield us from them; but they overrun us nevertheless. We know, as James Baldwin observed about racism, that injustice abounds, but we must never accept injustice as commonplace.[9] *That* knowledge takes us into spiritual struggle.

So here is the human condition: We care a great deal about living but our lives can be taken in a flash by accident, illness, or a random act of violence. We want to believe, but doubt is present even in the moments we embrace God. We long to be whole, but we are put at risk by the unanticipated: the loss of a child, of a job, of a relationship, of our own health. To protect ourselves, we become guarded, even suspicious; we withdraw— sometimes for good reason. After all, every day our fears are reinforced as we are barraged with the misfortunes and misdeeds of others—on the national and local news, and from the gossip friends relay to us in the hallway at work. It's easy to become tainted by this constant exposure to the seamy side and perplexing uncertainties of life; but when—surely—we are wary and negative, we lose our spiritual mooring.

The many and sometimes ugly injustices of the world bring us to spiritual struggle.

3. The Struggle with Insincerity

For more than a quarter-century, I have been at the top of relatively large institutions of higher learning. As I reflect on those years, I see remarkable achievements—organizational and individual. But I also see vividly the treacheries of everyday people in the workplace—as they maneuver for power, security, recognition, advancement, retribution. Rarely are these treacheries naked. Those involved (usually several people attempting to do each other in) may speak kindly to each other, even swear friendship and loyalty. But their blades are long, and they show little hesitation to drive them into the backs of their associates! It is often said: There are no more ruthless politics than campus politics.

I received a long letter from a future subordinate a week or so before I began a new job as president of a college. In it, she graciously pledged steadfast loyalty, spoke with admiration, and characterized my coming to campus as an "extraordinary opportunity for her to learn." She also described certain conspiratorial acts under way to ensure that I had early failures—the acts, of course, of named and unnamed *others*. I was astonished by the scope and gravity of her revelations but pleased with this gesture of support.

Soon after my arrival, the editor of the local newspaper shared with me a concern that a high-ranking official of the college had attempted to have the paper publish what his researchers found to be untrue and slanderous reports about me. Who was this person? It was none other than my "loyal" subordinate letter writer!

Of course, I felt betrayed. It took some effort to keep me from suspecting everyone in my new cabinet of disingenuous conduct.

Insincerity can lead to an insidious form of spiritual struggle. And it's easy to fall into. We live in a world where, every day, people say they care, but their actions may not conform to their verbal assurances. Friends say they care, loved ones say they care, colleagues say they care, even strangers say they care. But, many images come before us that cast doubt upon the sincerity, the potency, and the endurance of these expressions of care. Words of support when coupled with failure to follow through—no matter what the reason—can bring us to spiritual struggle with insincerity. Perhaps those around us mean to act consistently with their assurances; perhaps they don't. The effect is the same. Trust is breached, and breaches of trust strike at the heart of spiritual well-being because they get in the way of open, affirming relationships that are key to spiritual health.

We only have to be patients for a short time to recognize that care words can lead to feelings of disappointment, even betrayal. Practitioners often use them for encouragement, though they themselves may have little genuine empathy with us. We and our families sometimes thrive on these words and, other times, feel violated by them.

My wife developed a close friendship with her physician several years ago. They shared a common interest in community theater.

When my wife came down with the symptoms of a strep throat while starring in a musical, she called her for help. "I'll do what I can," she was told. "Come in early tomorrow morning." She did, but the examination seemed hurried and incomplete. She did leave with a prescription, but also dismayed. On her way back to the reception area, she noticed her friend's schedule for the day. There, her name was—with many others—typed in for "six minutes"!

When the prescription turned out to be ineffective, she was flooded with feelings of disappointment, even disillusionment. Words of care hadn't been translated into actions of care.

These episodes that we all have in life cause us to doubt the sincerity of those about us—even those committed by profession and relationship to aid us. They erode our sense of well-being and breed distrust.

And distrust is a seedbed of spiritual malaise.

4. The Struggle with Inauthenticity

The ultimate source of spiritual struggle comes from a commonly expressed desire to live consistently with our deeply embedded and most cherished ideals. Most people in our study said they had set out to make their hopes and aspirations reality. By midlife, however, they realized how difficult this is to do.

I began to understand the true proportions of this form of spiritual struggle when I met Jack at a conference of social workers in Southern California some years ago.

Jack and I were copresenters. He appeared to be a "together" man, a model of emotional and spiritual health.

I was taken aback when he called several months later to seek counsel about his spiritual struggle. His wasn't a struggle with belief or denominational particulars; it was the kind most of us experience at that point in life when we pause to ask what we're doing, where we're going—and why.

As he related, he was caught between a commitment to "be there" for all of his clients and a personal financial crisis. He found himself—for the first time in his career—in the position where he had to turn away clients in pain who couldn't meet their fee obligations. Money now was beginning to govern his practice. He was conflicted! He felt spiritually adrift.

Jack's struggle was to live out faithfully the convictions that propelled him into the field of counseling years before. Put simply: He was repulsed by hypocrisy in his life.

He wanted his work to be consistent with his innermost values and aspirations. He wanted, above all, to feel at home with himself—in his work as well as in his private life. He desired the strength that authenticity brings to all of life.

Nevertheless, he was damned if he didn't see therapy as a business, and, of course, damned if he did. This is a prevalent form of spiritual struggle: being caught between two opposing moral choices. As I expected, Jack, an extraordinarily caring and sensitive man, resolved his struggle through a painful restructure of his finances, trading down cars and office space. A difficult but laudable decision!

Like Jack, most people long to carry on their lives in tune with their ideals. They desire a touchpoint with God, reassurance that they are on the right path. They seek a vision that will energize them and integrate all of the facets of their lives.

But, we live in a world where Jack's solution is against the stream. Most cover their own needs first and rationalize their choices later. Of course, *Jack was in a privileged position. He had a choice!* Sometimes, resolution is not in our control. Decisions of others and unforeseen events often determine our life course. We all can be ambushed by jealousy, mean-spiritedness, selfishness, misunderstanding, misfortune. We all can be caught up in megachange: economic downturns, office power plays, and the like. We all may struggle to live out our ideals.

Inauthenticity blocks us from sustained spiritual well-being. It prevents us from sealing our relationships with "self" and with others.

So here, in a few words, is why we struggle spiritually. We find it difficult to

- break the hold of insecurity
- cope with injustice
- reconcile ourselves with insincerity
- put our beliefs and values consistently into action

Generally, our traditions have taught us few effective strategies for getting these things accomplished—and so, rarely have we discovered where the power resides that could pull us out of struggle, and rarely have we used that power.

II

Breaking from "The Struggles"

O ur research reveals that vital connections—with God, with the sacred, with one's faith tradition, and with others—position searchers to experience spiritual well-being. These connections are made and sealed through these commitments: trust, belief, empathy, and centered reflection.

Magical moments, illuminations of the human spirit, "soul to soul" dialogues with partners, conversations with God—these are not uncommon even in the twenty-first century. In fact, people speak daily of these experiences. What are their origins? They could be passed off as the products of overactive imagination or undiscerning belief—naïveté. But most people—those who are religious, even those who profess no faith—recount them to be bona fide *spiritual* encounters.

Years ago, during the Cold War, I interviewed Edward Teller, "the father of the hydrogen bomb," well-known humanist and scientist. I recall his monumental reflection: "I'm certain we (Americans) will prevail. When you stifle human creativity, *the human spirit*, you will never match the achievements of those who live and work in freedom." Clearly, he recognized a spirit that even the most infamous tyrants and crushing systems have not been able to suppress.

In moments when people say they are attuned to the spirit, to their inner selves, to the sacred, to what is "Greater," to God, they believe they can overcome destructive struggle, get beyond injustice, insincerity, insecurity, even inauthenticity. Eighty-six percent of focus group participants indicated that they know that if they live guided by their inner spirit, consistent with their deeply held values and hopes, they will have enduring well-being. But what does such a life look like? What is the source of spiritual power? How can life struggles be kept from eroding away spiritual well-being? How is connectedness nurtured? *These* are the million-dollar questions.

Our research has identified several vital life commitments that correlate strongly with spiritual well-being. Those who make these life commitments invariably report answers to these difficult questions and the release into their everyday lives of the power of Scend.

These *Commitments*, when habitual, transport people from doubt and negativity to confidence and optimism, from disconnection and struggling to vital connection and well-being.[1] They build upon one another, and they are most potent when they are consciously recognized and celebrated.

Commitment 1: Build Authentic Relationships (Trust)

Spiritual well-being, by definition, begins in community—through healing, empowering, confirming, intuitive relationships—with others, with the sacred, with God, with our inner selves. For some, these bonds are sacramental; for others, they are based simply on openness and care. Spiritual relationships, we found in virtually every case, are built from integrity, out of vulnerability, and through embrace—in a word, from trust.[2] In the language of Jesus, whoever

---

Five Commitments: Spiritual Well-Being*

Spirituality

Commitment 5: Go Forward with Spirit (Inspiration)

Commitment 4: Make the Inside Connection (Centered Reflection)

Commitment 3: Listen with the Heart (Empathy)

Commitment 2: Respond to the Quiet Voice Within (Belief)

Commitment 1: Build Authentic Relationships (Trust)

*See Appendix E for survey data; see chapter 3 for details about Commitment 5.

"is faithful in that which is least is faithful in that which is most" (Luke 16:10).

Those surveyed who indicated they strongly agreed they were spiritually satisfied consistently scored high on loyalty and fidelity—and they were least likely to say they would give up an important relationship for personal gain, even for a million dollars. They see the integral connection between keeping relationships secure and achieving spiritual well-being. Typically, they indicated their "finest expression is to love someone" (Question 24).

It is widely understood that sustained, close relationships are a primary source of happiness—more significant than income, job, and social status. And, they are foundational to spiritual well-being. As early as the second century C.E., Christians recognized that family is where salvation is worked out.[3] Yet, relationships are so easily and commonly put at risk or abandoned entirely. This story has been told in many versions by many people.

I had lunch recently with Stuart, a prominent executive known for his business acumen and great marriage. We spoke of common interests, mainly of our diets and wellness plans. As the check arrived and we disputed who would pick it up, a sudden, momentary expression of hurt contorted his otherwise relaxed countenance. "Let's stay here a minute longer," I insisted. "I don't think you're ready to leave. You need to tell me what's going on in your life." He did!

Known to virtually no one in the community, he had just received final divorce papers.

Somewhat embarrassed, he revealed that his very comfortable marriage of seventeen years had gone from happy and secure to total disintegration in a matter of months. He pleaded with her to stay, he confided, but that was not to be. She had told the therapist in their final joint session, "I want to start over again. There's no sense in talking further."

My mind flashed back to a party at their home several months before. It had been my most recent encounter with them as a couple. I recall her eyes as she and Stuart danced in the living room—darting about with enticement and sexual energy. I wondered then, "What does it mean?" I know now she was not, as he apparently supposed, settled in to married life—all other appearances aside.

It is a virtual cliché to say: Life lived above destructive struggle can't be had if there's inner unrest, a wandering eye, energized flirtations, a continuous scan of the world for better opportunities, a look for greener pastures. But human behavior so frequently denies this.

Of course, loyalty, integrity, honesty are not, in the actual practice of life, so easily charted. Among the questions asked of applicants to highly selective universities are these: Do you have integrity? Are you honest? Of course, the interviewers are not seeking yes or no answers. They want to determine whether the potential student is trustworthy—*and* sees the ambiguities that are involved.

There are many possible ways to satisfy these questioners that we have integrity *and* see the complexities of life. We could impress them by saying that we don't spend money easily because we are faithful to the provider of our funds and to our own commitment to be prudent. We could assure them that we are honest, except in extraordinary cases when being entirely honest could lead to a greater moral failure: the wrongful taking of a life, the persecution of innocent people, etc. We could tell them we realize integrity is stronger once tested—when it comes out of the crucible of life.

There are ambiguities and complexities in trust as well, but, almost universally, people hold loyalty to be foundational to the virtuous life. Of course, living in a complex world can test anyone's resolve to speak and act consistently from trust. And, there are times when fidelity is powerfully challenged through life-defining events. Most people come to a fork in the road at some point in life where they are tested. My turn came on a cold day in the Windy City when I became president of a college in Chicagoland.

Not long after I assumed office, I began a campaign of campus beautification. First on the agenda was painting the exteriors of several buildings. Bids were received from local contractors and the "lowest and best" was awarded the contract. To my surprise and consternation, the only work that was completed was the application of a thin coat of paint on the peeling, blistered surface of the administration building.

Sufficiently agitated, I called the contractor. His response astonished me. It was entirely beyond any I'd ever heard. "No," he growled, "I'm not going to paint the buildings your way, because then you wouldn't hire me next year to paint them again." Later reflection told me he actually wasn't crazy, just corrupt. He had a nice deal! He could be the annual low bidder, assuring him the job in perpetuity; and he could carry most of our payment dollars straight to his bank account.

My sharp and immediate response apparently took him off guard. "No," I insisted, "paint the buildings according to our specs or no money!"

He paused as if speechless and then thundered: "You'll pay for this!"

Later, I was told this man was a kingpin of organized crime, and that, most likely, my life was in danger—a chilling revelation. But I felt I had no choice. Bowing to his demand would shatter me as a moral person; it was out of the question. In time, we retained another contractor and the buildings were painted. Fortunately, I never heard again from the first contractor. I felt I had done what was valued morally, *in its own right,* without diminishing any other value or any other one. Acting as though invulnerable, to do what is right despite evident vulnerability, whatever the consequences, brings us in touch with our inner strength and positions us to act with integrity in all our dealings.

There also are times when relationships are secured *through* vulnerability. Being vulnerable to those who are close actually builds intuitive bonds. But it isn't easy. Research psychologists have found that a single negative experience with another person almost invariably unravels positive feelings received from many affirming interactions.[4] In short, humans are predisposed against vulnerability!

Over millennia, humans have survived by giving bad events far more weight than good ones, and for good reason. Seeing all opportunities as potentially enhancing can lead to disaster. Some may be truly destructive. So most are wary of letting others see their soft side. We strive to be—or, at least, to appear—invulnerable, even to ourselves.

Nevertheless, here's what our research shows: Those who take measured risks and reach out to others in openness are more likely to experience spiritual well-being, especially those who take the even greater risk of finding their authentic selves (the locus of deeply embedded hopes, beliefs, and values).

The stories told in this book usually are about extraordinary happenings and about exceptional people doing exceptional things—the "best of the best." Here, garden-variety accounts are appropriate. The vulnerability upon which spiritual life is built is expressed customarily in small gestures, "random acts of kindness"—like the opening of flowers in a meadow at daybreak. A friend revealing he has been an alcoholic and is still quite fragile—not the strong man she thought he was; a neighbor lady who blows snow off the sidewalk in the winter for an elderly man because she cares; a caseworker reporting to the clinic to extend care with a face distorted by Bell's Palsy; those who risk rejection and undermine their carefully crafted images to support friends—all those times when common folks reach out in vulnerability and do selfless acts for the betterment of others.

Relationships and trust are remarkably built and sustained when people go against their instincts and are *open* (though not defenseless) to partners in life (mates, parents, children, friends, associates). Certainly, most people have suffered disappointment, even disillusionment; perhaps they have had to close down for safety and sanity. *Healthy, sustaining relationships, however, come through bonding with those who frame our existence—* indeed, with all those whose lives intersect ours—based on integrity and in the face of risk.

Most of us get this message some time in life that we have to connect with significant others. We are, above all, social animals, and we need support, confirmation, enrichment, connection. Even in the Texas Hill Country, where highly successful and individualistic people have moved to live sequestered on ranches tens to thousands of acres in size, most everyone has found it necessary to seek out "neighbors" to solve problems of water supply, traffic, degradation of the landscape, youth violence, light pollution, and the like.

As they have bonded with those about them through churches and political movements, they have found purpose and social power. And, they say, they have become spiritually enriched.

Typically, moderns travel in the opposite direction, trapped in lifestyles that *weaken* connections and community ties: driving encased in their cars; living in rows of houses that are all basically the same; working out of closed spaces; holding neighbors at bay, communicating with them at a distance—via the Internet and cell phones, from our private offices and protected compounds. It's common to move away from family, watch TV *alone*, play solitaire on our laptops, shop by catalog and computer. *Who we are in relation to others these days is not so much personal as much as it is commercial.* This is why many are lonely, some futureless—even among our affluent citizenry.

Our research shows that separation from others is not conducive to spiritual health. It leads people to struggle with insecurity, even inauthenticity. Worse, in an insulated state, individuals can slip from isolation to alienation—self-defeating estrangement from others and from themselves.

Loneliness can be hurtful; alienation debilitates.

How does this slide occur? A story from our legendary past clarifies how.

> Years ago, the collector of *The Jack Tales*—folklorist Richard Chase, my companion on a train from Los Angeles to Santa Barbara—led me beyond the beanstalk saga of our childhood into Jack's doings in the mountains of Carolina and, more important, to an uncommon insight into the common experience we often call "alienation" (the root of inauthenticity).
>
> Jack was a young farmer, the writer noted. He was moving west with his kin into the foothills. They were clearing "new ground" so that they could extend their land and make a better living. This very understandable and peaceful journey brought them into direct

confrontation with backwoods people, very different people!

In the story, Chase relates, the people Jack and his brothers encounter actually came from the same English stock, but they had forged an entirely different culture based on mountain living. To Jack, they were strangers—soon adversaries. They couldn't be trusted and certainly not befriended. Some were, as he imagined them, ruthless and savage—two-headed giants!

As *The Jack Tales* unfold, we learn more about Jack's deep fear of these monsters of the forest. We learn that Jack was anxiety-ridden because he didn't feel safe with the people up the road. He was in *their* world; and he wasn't wanted. In fact, his new-found enemies were determined to get rid of him and his brothers. And, so the stories go, he schemed to get rid of them.

When we reduce these tales from myth to reality, we realize that Jack had slipped from the dread, the anxiety of feeling isolated in a new locale, to the full-blown *alienation* of being in a foreign land among hostile strangers. He had lost his moorings and, soon, his sense of self. Of course, though not recognized in *The Jack Tales*,[5] his backwoods adversaries felt the very same way. After all, it was *their* world that the intruders—Jack and his brothers—had entered intent upon changing.

As Jack and his kin—and his adversaries—experienced their foundations shifting, they didn't feel "at home"—safe—any longer. They were in a dangerous world; they were displaced persons; they were powerless. That is alienation—separation from all things familiar that grant us security and authenticity resulting in a crippling feeling of apprehension—angst.

People today, like Jack and his brothers, come and cut in our forest; they make our backyards unfamiliar worlds. They can bring us to social bankruptcy, as if we have relocated to a strange land. When we suspect intruders are not operating with our well-being in mind, we suffer anxiety—not only from separation *from others and from familiar places* but *from our very selves.* To salvage meaning and purpose, many put their life's energy into climbing up the power/security ladder, buying houses of greater size, achieving envied lifestyles. But when these aspirations are reached, people are no more secure, no more in tune with themselves, no more satisfied than they were before. Their search is inadequate to the task of overcoming the dread of alienation!

The pathway to security is commonly experienced as circuitous—difficult to follow, taking us in circles. In fact, it may be quite simple to follow. I love this Buddha story:

> One day, Buddha came across an ascetic, presumably a monk, who had practiced a very austere, self-denying lifestyle for years. The Buddha asked him, "What did you get for all your effort and sacrifice?"
>
> Proudly, the ascetic replied, "Now I can cross the river by walking on the water."
>
> The Buddha was not impressed. He pointed out that self-denial had yielded very little. "I, too, can cross the river," he admonished, "by ferry and for just one penny."

What is the lesson? We can go far out of our way to achieve a prized goal, but our efforts may take us no farther than what is available to us already. The simple way to cross the river may well be available readily: *reaching out to embrace those who intersect our life paths, not treating them as strangers and adversaries.* Since September 11, 2001, according to the National Opinion Research Center, the percentage of people who "feel others are helpful" is reported to be on a trendline up. Reaching out and building relationships based on transparency, vulnerability, and embrace—connecting even with "intruders"—keeps people from alienation, grants them inner strength, and frees them from spiritual struggle.

This is accomplished by looking past judging others to accepting them, past dominating to embracing them. *When people reach out to others, they find they are at peace with themselves.* If Jack and his brothers had taken apple pies up the road to their new neighbors instead of brandishing axes, they would have affirmed who they were, avoided needless struggle, and escaped alienation.

The modern world is hard-edged, patched together by cold words: the words of legal contracts, the words of our employers' policies and procedures, the words of clichés and empty greetings, even words that are "little white lies." Taking cold words and turning them into warm words—words of care and concern—overcomes alienation, from others and from self.

Strong relationships keep us from sliding into alienation and inauthenticity and, therefore, into spiritual struggle. Those who remain committed to their community of faith, who experience with fellow parishioners God's grace, who work for reconciliation, who reach out even to those pulling away, tranScend the abyss of separation. They are on the road away from alienation toward spiritual well-being.

Commitment 2: Respond to the Quiet Voice Within (Belief)

So often, given the explosion of sects and the omnipresence of the televangelists and their ilk, when people search for meaning, connectedness, freedom from struggle, and ultimate significance, they end up under the spell of a compelling personality or cultic belief. They seek "truth" and truthtellers that can stand the challenges of cynicism and the grit in everyday living. When we scan the spiritual landscape, however, we discover that enduring spiritual strength rarely comes through the teachings of charismatic religious leaders. The ups and downs of their converts bear vivid testimony to this fact. The founders and prophets of the world's great religions, in fact, were not likely spellbinders. They were ordinary people who responded powerfully to a compelling voice within: the nomad Abraham; the illiterate Muhammad; the peasant girl in Bethlehem, Mary; the lowly carpenter, Jesus; the voluntarily impoverished Buddha. And in each faith tradition, through sacred scripture, worship, singing, praying or meditating, and celebrating sacraments, ordinary people hear the voice of God and become spiritually whole.

The everyday illuminations that are central to spiritual life invariably come from within. This is consistent with the recent findings of scientists that "the deepest origins of religion are based in mystical experience"[6] and with Paul's observation that "with the heart one believes unto righteousness" (Rom. 10:10).

Leaders of virtually all of the world's religious traditions teach that God is heard through people's *souls*. Stories of faith resonate *in the heart*; followers are moved by ceremony *to well up inside*; they *stand in awe of* God's magnificent expressions in nature; God responds to their prayers through that *"quiet voice within."*

The faithful seek healing in Christianity (salvation), wisdom in Buddhism (enlightenment), liberation from the cycle of misery in Hinduism (nirvana), oneness with God and his people in Judaism (sanctification), conformity to the will of God in Islam (submission)—all granted, not as thunderbolts from another world, *but as revelations from within*. Sometimes, these revelations are translated through religious leaders, sometimes through those outside religious traditions, even through the profane.

> I had just moved to Ohio. It was April Fool's Day, but there was no fooling about the weather: cold and bleak.
>
> Our family decided to go out for dinner to the restaurant guide's best spot. There, we found a party in progress. To our delight, we were included immediately.
>
> The host was Tom, a local car dealer—a deal-maker supreme, earthy, somewhat rough around the edges, but altogether winsome, even inspiring.
>
> As we became friends, I discovered his "other side"— the real Tom. When our mutual friend, a banker, was in his last months of fighting against a fatal cancer, Tom called

him each morning at 8:00 a.m. to encourage him and raise his spirits for the difficult day ahead.

Tom wasn't a renowned theologian; he wasn't an elder in a church; he wasn't even a church member. But he heard a voice inside telling him to reach out to our dying friend. He listened to God's voice. It gave to him, as well as to those about him—certainly our banker friend—a wondrous sense of well-being, a confidence that he was on the right side in life.

Whatever their faith commitment, people we surveyed consistently reported that when they *listened to the God Within*, gnawing emptiness dissolved; a sense of well-being was theirs. Heeding the voice inside bestows both emotional and spiritual security, they reported. We can conclude, therefore, that if people reorder their spiritual lives—from the search for messages from a god outside *to openness to the constant God Within*—they will be positioned to surge forward to well-being.

Augustine captured this essential nearly seventeen centuries ago:

And what place is there...in me into which my God can come, even He who made heaven and earth?...Is there anything in me, O Lord my God, that can contain Thee?...in Thee, from whom are all things, by whom are all things, in whom...are all things?[7]

Typically, when the word *belief* is used, modern hearers think of doctrine, dogma, some specific set of "truths." That is because moderns have been influenced first by Greek thought and lately by the world of science to search out laws, facts, theories that hold true. As it turns out, *belief*—traditionally and foundationally—is expressing faith.[8] After all, no two people tell a story, see the world, express surely ultimate guiding principles precisely the same way. Analysis of the physical world leads to hypotheses—demonstrated facts. But the inner world is accessed quite differently. Religious dogmas, in other words, only lead to grand cul-de-sacs. Whole faith transports believers to inner strength and confidence.[9]

George Gallup, Jr.'s, studies have shown that the faithful—whatever their tradition—are those who most often stay free of destructive social deviance, support noble causes, enjoy life satisfaction[10]—not because of the superiority of their theology, but by the power of their faith commitments.

How can people live by faith in a nation where civic health is in such evident decline? How can they live by faith when they are encumbered by responsibilities, chores, and obligations? How can they be spiritually whole thrashing about in unfamiliar waters? How can they glide forward when their movements are complicated, unnatural, and discombobulated and when their minds are astir and their emotions aflame? The answer is spiritual streamlining.

In the water, streamlining is pushing off of a firm poolside, stretching out, reaching arms and hands as one toward a destination, relaxed and gliding as far as initial breath and thrust can carry. With this smooth and powerful start, competitive swimmers launch themselves—effortlessly and gracefully.

In the spiritual domain, streamlining is pushing off from a firm foundation—one's faith community, deeply embedded values, spiritual center.[11] And it's being goal-directed, having purpose in life, remaining confident and under control while moving toward a clear destination. There's no thrashing about because streamlining eliminates unnecessary strokes, minimizing fear and anxiety that wreak havoc by pulling the overcommitted into a vortex of struggle. In a word, spiritual streamlining is *simplifying* living.

The prerequisites to streamlining—in both swimming and spirituality—are the same:

- knowing where you want to go and heading directly there
- pushing off relaxed, confident, and together, certain you will reach your destination

- using effective and economical strokes that reduce resistance and exertion and propel you forward with strength and endurance
- gliding along—as if on a great wave—through Scend, the power of the Spirit

Focus group believers tell of these results: experiencing oneness with their environment; having a strong sense of direction; living the whoosh of effortless achievement (Flow),[12] cutting through resistance; building a toned and relaxed spiritual disposition; realizing "the peace that passes all understanding." How does streamlining occur?

Patti revealed "Step One" when she spoke out in an informal session after the first of the year. Our discussion had centered on our New Year's resolutions and our poor record of achieving them. She turned the conversation on end with this surprising pronouncement: "Here's my resolution: I'm going to do *less* each day this year until I get to the point where only essential things get done!"

Exactly what does she intend to jettison? "All meetings where my presence makes no real difference, all trips to malls and stores for things I'll probably end up putting away or giving to charity, all chores that are not needed for the family's health and happiness, all mind-numbing TV-watching—*everything* I do that doesn't take me directly to where I want to go, everything I do that isn't truly enriching for my family and others."

Patti is off and running and in the right direction. She is streamlining!

When believers reduce their many pursuits to achieving the primary, everyday goal of spiritual well-being, *they make key lifestyle changes, and, when this life reorientation becomes habitual, they experience a new level of living.* Specifically, they separate out what wins the day from what occupies time. They get a new perspective on life choices and become willing to be less and not more, even *have* less and not more. They find what is fixed and firm in life and vault from it—with clear purpose and direction. They yearn to live freely, as the Spirit guides. Above all, they strive to have an open mind.

Several years ago, I was host for a television special featuring respected enviro-journalists. I recall the dramatic story of Mark Schleifstein of the *New Orleans Times-Picayune*. He told about his struggle to have published his Pulitzer prize-winning story concerning oceans on the verge of ecocollapse. The publisher could see nothing compelling in the piece, Mark recounted, until he was told that his favorite restaurant, the famous Commanders Palace, was out of red fish—perhaps forever! "Print the story," exclaimed the publisher.

Each person sees *one's own* world, not *the* world, because one's ears and eyes have filters and lenses. And when anxieties arise, invariably distortion increases. So now, confused by changing landscapes and overrun by instantaneous transmission of popular culture, by the continuous introduction of new technologies, the increasing mobility of people planetwide, destabilizing social structures everywhere, and unforeseen enemies on multiple fronts, people in droves close down their minds and clutch tenaciously to adopted explanations of life—especially religious explanations in the form of beliefs, "truths," doctrines.

Unfortunately, these pat explanations that lead people to thinking they are right and, therefore, secure, simultaneously block connections with others, taking away security. Typically, as they say in the South, when folks get crosswise with others, they don't stay together—at least not for long. Knowing this, most seek out only certain chat rooms and listen to the talk radio that speaks their language of life—their politics, their prejudices. This is why many burn bridges, abandon friends. Why are so many convinced that they are in the right? Perhaps they have had a riveting experience or been entranced by a consuming personality—a star, a televangelist, a powerful figure. Most often, it's because their "truths" do some very important things for them: They justify their behavior, past and present, and their lifestyle, especially their prized views; and they help take the gray issues in life and make them black and white. They provide the combination that opens up the mystery of who are the bad guys and who are the good guys. They may even make some people part of an elite group, "the children of the truth"! It's intoxicating to know "the truth" and be part of the selected family of the truth. Unfortunately, "truths"—even religious truths—lead away from spirituality. They, in fact, block out messages from the God Within.

It may be said that the more adamant a person is that he is right, the more likely it is he is not. (Of course, truth can stand on its own feet—it doesn't require insistence.) Also, it can be said that the more dogmatic a person is, the farther he is likely to move from others and so from spiritual health.

These assertions become obvious when we have the luxury to look back to those before or who are at a distance. Few would deny that well-meaning "truthbearers"—no, "truthhurlers"—have used class, gender, race, and belief to mistreat and suppress others, from the Inquisition to modern genocides and terrorism. And few would deny that it has become increasingly difficult to reach out to others in a world in which religious markers of identity are the most divisive of all differences.[13] In any case, it's more difficult to view the prisons of our own minds than the prisons of those about us.

I found myself at a business luncheon a number of years ago with Harold, the owner of a small manufacturing company. He had just returned from a church conference on "How to Bring Christian Principles into the Workplace." Our conversation held my total attention. His was an amazing story to me, because Harold prides himself on being a spiritual leader.

> For twenty-two years, Harold had employed Richard—most recently as his executive vice president—who, he related, had taken his business from less than $100,000 in annual sales to more than $100 million. "He

has made me a rich man," Harold confided, "but I had to let him go this morning. It was the hardest decision I've ever had to make."

"I'm sure it was," I reflected, "but why?"

His response was immediate and unqualified: "I can't have a shop pleasing to God run by a man like Richard."

"What did he do?" I inquired with eager anticipation.

"I've warned him for a year," he responded, "that his son is an embarrassment to him and to our company. Now, he heads up a gay rights organization. Gays and God don't mix."

My mind was racing and my heart heavy as I reflected on what this man was telling me. Who knows how great the harm to Richard and his family that will result from this extraordinarily precipitous and overreaching action! Who knows the fear that workers in his plant will feel when they hear about the owner's callous act!

I began the process of exposing the destructiveness of my lunch partner's closed-minded decision—not so much to Richard or to the business—but to Harold himself. To be right *spiritually*, he committed a terrible spiritual wrong. What an irony! Unfortunately, I didn't get far.

Closed minds and rank prejudice not only prevent bonding with others, they lead otherwise good people to act deplorably, to demonize those with different worldviews and lifestyles, and tune out the God who is trying to speak to their heart. Ultimately, they render legitimate beliefs illegitimate and narrow the circle of those they trust—whom they consider as friends and associates. With closed minds, people actually want their news, sermons, political rhetoric, even college lectures to *confirm* their established views of the world rather than provide new insights. *Closed minds assure us we're right, but at the expense of healing relationships that make us right.*

While religious leaders for generations have issued strong admonitions against closed-minded judgment of others—lest one be judged, lest one attempt to avoid self-examination, lest one escape remorse, lest one set oneself up as God—narrow-minded believers have projected themselves routinely as the ultimate judges of who is in and who is out, bound for heaven or discharged to hell! Movements within Islam, Judaism, and Christianity—for centuries and in this hour—provide dramatic testimonials to this assertion.

So here is a test to discover whether we have fallen prey to destructive bias:

- Have our beliefs closed off the opportunity of sharing with others who have come into our lives?
- Are our encounters with others bias-free?
- Will the choices we make today bring us closer to others?
- How will they appear a year from now: noble or prejudicial?

We find that those who profess spiritual well-being are not limited by bias. They seek out stories of faith and inspiration; read the scriptures and works of edification; reflect on the life of Christ; contemplate nature's grandeur and power; celebrate great human expression—through the arts, young children, acts of kindness, ennobling literature, exemplary conduct. Above all, they reach out to others in need, and they give up the very real pleasure of being self-righteous.

Commitment 3: Listen with the Heart (Empathy)

America has become a nation of great diversity. This has become, virtually, a trite statement. The 2000 census revealed that most every city and town in America has undergone sweeping demographic change in the decades that closed out the twentieth century. Diversity in national origin, race, political persuasion—certainly religion—now separates our experience of community from that of past generations. Sometimes, Americans celebrate this newfound pluralism. But many have responded by insulating themselves from neighbors and fellow citizens, holding themselves back, unknowingly, from spiritual growth, leading themselves to spiritual struggle. Believers speak, especially in church, of love and respect for neighbors, but, so often, they relate only to the look-alikes around them. It's difficult to bridge the gap between races and cultures. Americans learned a hard lesson in the twentieth century and had it reinforced powerfully on September 11, 2001: We can't bring most others to our belief system—by persuasion, or even by force.

After the Second World War, there was a nearly universal expectation that all peoples and nations would work together for humanity's good and, in the United States, that all Americans would achieve social equity. The ecumenical movement was well under way. But, the century ended with ethnic strife on every continent and with great lifestyle disparities. And there were more denominations, not fewer. In the new century, diabolical acts of terrorism and persistent, embittered regional conflicts have dashed remaining hopes for world peace and unity.

How can individuals bond with those about them? Not through common belief—that is unlikely—but by empathy.[14] Empathy is the miracle potion! It draws others in. It is the catalyst that enables people of all backgrounds to form care communities, communities that enrich the common experience and expand all spirits.

> Recently, I watched my granddaughter play softball: two teams of ten, in different-colored uniforms, from separate parts of town, all five or six years old, all happy to be together.

> They came to have fun, but it wasn't long before parents' comments were in the air, revealing other agendas: winning, making certain their "prospect" was given the proper chance to show her stuff, getting the correct stance and swing down pat—You've been there! You've felt the tension, or your children have!

> By inning two, cross-team parent conversations had all but ceased. Camaraderie—all twenty girls enjoying a

Saturday morning together, learning what it means to be on a team, gaining a playing skill here and there—had gone by the boards. By the game's end, some were jubilant, others despondent.

Surely, I conjectured to myself, fostering empathy would have led to a different outcome. We could bring all parents and players together *before* each game to meet each other, hear about the other Suzies on the field and focus on our mutual hope: that all the girls would enjoy the experience, take away valuable lessons of teamwork and playing—and be friends, and that all parents encourage all the players. We *could* build strong bonds—among losers as well as winners. And we *all* could have had a more pleasurable Saturday morning!

In the larger world, when *communities of care* are formed, the forces of alienation that pull people into spiritual struggle are neutralized. Caregivers reach out to others, no matter how different they may be; they build intimate affiliations so all can enter—as they say of Chicago's Wrigley Field: the "Friendly Confines" where we know "whose side we're on because we're all on the same side." Put simply: The catalyst for bonding is empathy.

For some, empathy comes naturally.[15] Others less empathic have to follow the lead of actors who seek the truth of the characters they play by studying their words and movements, feeling their emotions, taking on—as the actors' own—their life perspectives and longings. Many rehearsals are required to make the shift from theirs to their characters' egos. So it is with bonding with others through empathy. It takes the special effort of setting aside one's own interests for those of another until empathic behavior is second nature. The events of September 11, 2001, reveal that most people are capable of such altruistic conduct. New York City's police and fire services amazed the world with their unrestrained commitment that day and in the months that followed.

Empathy begins with mimicking but it triumphs through compassion—getting inside the skin of others to fathom their needs and hopes, share their struggles,[16] feel their hurts, hear their cry for dignity, and then act accordingly.

Some time ago, I was visiting a former student in Philadelphia who was then attending the Wharton School. Mike and his wife, Stacy, were waiting at the airport when I arrived late at night. On our way to their home, his old Volvo station wagon ran out of gas. It was near midnight. We were marooned in the inner city. Confidently, Mike proposed: "Stay in the car with my wife. I'll find help. I think there's a bar a block or so up the street. I can hear noise coming from it."

Off he went. When he returned, it was with a rough-looking, somewhat inebriated man in a coonskin coat who assured us that he would take Mike to find gas and return shortly. Actually, I was afraid we'd never see Mike again.

After long, anxious moments, they did return—and with gas. When our stranger-rescuer had fueled the car, I stepped out and offered, "Here's $50 to cover your time and for being so good to us."

His response shamed me.

"I didn't do this for money," he protested. Then, he came close and embraced me. What a lesson!

This man displayed extraordinary compassion. I had placed a price tag on his magnanimous act and stripped him of his dignity. I treated him as an "other," but he identified with our plight and saw us as part of *his* community.[17]

Empathy opens us to others; it also will keep us from hurting others.

While in graduate school, I served a small church nestled in the hills of Pomona, California. The congregation was white; the surrounding neighbors were mostly African American and Hispanic. My assignment was to bring those about us into the fold

I began with a transformation of the property. The great front landscape of the church soon was populated by slides and swings and a volleyball court, and then scores of local children. The sign told more of welcome than of sermons of exclusion.

I was sitting atop our highest monkey bar one day, surveying the change and enjoying the laughter and delight. A little African American girl caught my attention. She waved goodbye as she set off for home across a neighbor's front yard. I was appalled to see an elderly white woman burst from her home and begin to strike the child with a broom amidst a hail of racial epithets.

The hurt I experienced was like the hurt of seeing my own child assaulted mindlessly. A glimpse of the African American experience—for the first time in my life—became mine.

The church grew; our neighbors became our congregation.

Empathy is the healing agent that connects very different people as soul mates. It steels them against fear and misdeeds. *Living through empathy is essential to overcoming the spiritual struggles of insecurity, insincerity, and certainly inauthenticity.*

What keeps people from showing empathy, feeling compassion? Surely one obstacle is loss and the resulting anxiety of vulnerability. When people suffer loss, they withdraw from others; they listen through their fears, not with their hearts. Everyone experiences loss, even early in life: loss of opportunity, loss of a loved one, loss of status, loss of power and control, loss of our feeling of invulnerability (as almost everyone experienced after September 11, 2001). All of these losses are weakening; some are debilitating. Unchecked, they lead to childlike fear and desperate dependence. They prevent otherwise strong people from breaking free of struggle. In fact, they deepen struggles with insecurity, insincerity, and injustice. Loss is a psycho-spiritual destroyer; its effects are difficult to shake, holding people captive in past pain and keeping them from being at peace with themselves. Loss often is compounded by guilt. "I didn't do enough for my loved one who has passed." "I didn't resolve issues before our separation." "I didn't tell him something very important—I love him." Loss brings one face to face with the inherent injustices of the world.

Loss also brings unsettling change; it reminds even the most devout that they are ultimately not in control. Loss—even relatively inconsequential loss—rudely calls to mind our own mortality.[18] Loss informs us that what is supposed to be, may not be. We are "supposed" to live safely and enjoy a long life. Loss tells us it can be otherwise. Most telling, loss often prevents us from reaching out to others.

When it's all said and done, loss immobilizes—loss of a loved one due to divorce, death, or a lifestyle conflict such as drug use or gender orientation change; loss of a job; loss of good health! Usually, these losses ambush; they catch most off guard. Even on the occasions when people know loss is coming (as in the case of a loved one with a terminal illness) or when there's been preparation for years (like the death of a parent), the feeling of being out of control, injured, isolated, and attacked—crushed—is triggered. Of course, each person reacts differently, depending on how involved one has been with the person or thing lost, or one's history with losses, or guilt about the relationship with the one lost. Reactions are individualized but, in so many ways, they *are* similar. Everyone feels betrayed, violated, wary, anxious—no matter the circumstance. And when we feel betrayed, we no longer listen with our heart. Instead, our focus is on our fears.

A number of observers have identified therapeutic "stages" that people undergo when they suffer profound loss: denial, anger, bargaining, depression, acceptance, and, finally, forbearance. Some think these stages come one after another and in this order. Others believe mourners pass in and out of them. Perhaps one can never get completely free of any of these responses to significant loss. *Grief can't be extinguished. It shouldn't be. It has to become integrated into life for people to experience ongoing spiritual well-being.* The challenge is how to do it.

Actor Vincent Price, a longtime friend, taught me one way. For most of life, especially young life, he argued, we are in the process of building connections—bonding with people about us and, in so doing, defining and redefining ourselves. Through this process, we flesh out who we are, and, as we do, we discover a larger meaning to our lives and fashion a greater self. Each loss—whether by divorce, estrangement, relocation, job separation, or death—therefore represents a stripping away of a piece of one's self. The first loss usually is the most telling because it interrupts the building process—often unexpectedly. It often shouts the last thing people want to hear: that they are starting down the back side of the hill of life. The death of my father was my first telling loss. I went from having a strong, resourceful parent who could command away adversity to having a dependent child to having a wilting void to no father, forever.

The first consequential loss begins the process of undoing years of framing and building. By old age, some become shells—experiencing the step-by-step reduction of their fully-formed selves. This may be a natural process through which we ready ourselves for our own demise, but nevertheless, it feels outrageously unnatural. It cramps the soul and keeps us in spiritual struggle. I recall Vincent's anguish that so many of his friends were no longer in the entertainment section of the paper but in the obituaries. He felt diminished. He *was* diminished!

Loss is made manageable when it is replaced with gain. Instead of denying loss or trying vainly to let go, new relationships have to be developed. It certainly is true that special relationships cannot be fully replaced. But the space they vacate in hearts and minds as they recede from active memory may be filled by new and different associations.

A focus group of senior citizens in California made this clear to me, especially one participant: Edgar.

Edgar had security and good health in his first year of retirement. He had a good marriage. Nevertheless, he attempted suicide. He drove his car onto a railroad track to end his anguish. Why? He felt alone; he felt empty. He had been a chief engineer in a large corporation; now, he did household chores and played golf with buddies. He had been a civic leader; now, he added one more body to weekly Kiwanis Club meetings. Nothing he did assuaged his overwhelming sense of meaninglessness. Edgar was in full struggle with inauthenticity.

After the train struck his car, he was sent unconscious to the hospital, but he survived. Through his hospital ordeal, he confided, "I came to realize that I could become a new Edgar." How?

Each day, Edgar sought out a new friend or found someone in need and provided a personal touch of assistance. When he was back to strength, he helped a new florist set up her business, he served as a tutor in English for Mexican immigrants, and he volunteered as an aide for a city councilman.

He now has, he told us with a broad smile, "a zest for life and a feeling in my soul that 'all is well.'"

Yes, relatives and friends fall away and he grieves over their loss. But these losses are made up "by my many gains."

Listening *with the heart* to those on the ride through life *with* us quiets struggle. When we listen with our hearts, we come to understand—wholly—our inner yearning and what our partners in life are telling us. Armed with this enlightenment, we can secure ourselves above destructive struggle, even the paralysis of insecurity.

So often, friends tell friends to listen *to* their hearts. But their hearts may reflect nothing more than momentary thoughts and desires, or they may be ruled by raging emotions or blinding fears or crippling events in our past. Our hearts may tell us that what *feels* right *is* right. More helpful is to listen *with* the heart. Hearts tell what is central to our lives. They usually are wiser than heads.

It's legendary that the indigenous people of the Americas used their exceptional sensitivity to nature to help them sense where danger loomed in forest and plain, as well as where sustenance could be found. It was their critical "sixth sense," their means of survival. In some tribes, like the Muscogee Nation, they used this special sense to connect with others. Their greeting is extraordinarily instructive: "I am you being me." We share, in other words, the same spirit. We are one.

Most of my focus group participants have expressed confidence that they have a sixth sense, the capacity to bond spiritually with others, to know where spiritual danger lurks and promise lies. They often report that they recall times when they have used their powers to get outside themselves and inside others. That's *listening with the heart*. These powers of spiritual sensitivity appear to be built into the human frame; they can connect individuals intuitively with those with whom they live and work; they can bring about spiritual wholeness.

Simpler relationships, like those with young children, teach us how we can hear with our hearts and find spiritual union.

> One day, I was waiting for my granddaughter, Sarah, to come out of preschool. As always, she ran to me and embraced me, but—this time—I could see that she was holding back tears.
>
> "What happened in school, sweetheart?" I asked.
>
> "Papa, Rachel said that I'm not her best friend anymore," she replied poignantly.
>
> Reflexively, I responded, "Well, you have other friends."
>
> NO! I had listened with my head, not with my heart. So I continued, "You are hurt, aren't you, darling? Let me hold you."
>
> I sat down on the sidewalk and we hugged each other for several minutes. Then, we could speak about what to do next—we had connected, heart to heart.

Of course, adult relationships are more complex, but the same principle applies: denying or brushing aside oneness with others is going in the wrong direction. Putting aside egos and scripted responses—listening and embracing with the heart—is taking the right step. Connecting emotionally (empathizing), physically (drawing close), and spiritually (nurturing the Scend within and among us) are the three essentials to listening with the heart. They bring resolution. Telling Sarah not to be hurt and discounting her feelings disconnected us. Moving to eye-to-eye level, then accepting her feelings, even adopting them as mine, cut to the core of her issue, opened the way to healing, and bonded us together. It is the ultimate validation that can be given to important others. "I share your hurt." "I feel your struggle." "I am you being me."

Listening with the heart triggers in lovers warmth and unbridled sexual expression, in friends and colleagues care and profound respect, and, with every companion, the deepest dimension of acceptance.

Listening with the heart enables those in tension to withstand the forces bent on pulling them apart. It leads to *spiritual* union. It ensures that we speak to each other from every possible perspective: heart and soul as well as mind and body. It makes two truly one.

Being joined from the heart with significant others also enables us to get off the path to *self*-fulfillment, a pathway that ultimately is divisive and unrewarding, and onto the broader road to *joint* fulfillment. It is, indeed, difficult to get beyond self. But it can be accomplished once we make a habit of feeling what important others feel, seeing the world through their eyes, reaching out through remarkable care and openness, once Scend carries us forward and we celebrate Scend expressed through others, once we make the sacred connection.

Those who listen with the heart typically hear the right answers and do the right things.

Virtually everyone has the capacity for sacred connection, whatever one's gender or role in life. And nearly all we interviewed said they wanted to live above relationship struggle; this included men as well as women. It is important to note that it is just as possible for a masculine man to be "softhearted" (open) as it is for a feminine woman to be hard-muscled. It turns out that being hard-muscled has value to some men and women; *but being "softhearted" is the foundation for building rich and intuitive relationships— for everyone!* Because of upbringing, perhaps genetic makeup, this may be more difficult for some. Even so, it can be nurtured in *all.* Speaking openly of needs and spelling out the care one seeks lead to heart-to-heart communication, *the most potent force in human experience.* We are—no question—weaker without it and immensely stronger with it. Those practiced in it insist it isn't hard to achieve. Virtually a glance, a gesture will do.

I learned this through an unforgettable encounter some years ago.

I was staying with friends in the seacoast town of Soverato in southern Italy. As on past occasions, family, friends, neighbors—twenty or so—gathered around my host's dinner table on my first night there—laughing, touching, enjoying each other's company, speaking of previous experiences together and what had transpired in the interim.

I noticed a different face, the face of a very shy young man. I was told that he was a distant relative from the north of Italy who had been so despondent, so overrun by stress, that he now didn't speak. He was invited to live with my friends to "find himself."

He was silent over nearly three hours of eating and celebrating. The next morning, as I was coming down the stairs, we made eye contact. Each day for a week, the same, but he didn't speak or even nod "hello." Nevertheless, I smiled at him and felt compelled to put my arms around him again and again, saying, "Caro." (I care.)

One afternoon, to my surprise, he motioned to me to come outside and go in his car with him. He remained silent and mysterious as we drove into town. When he parked, he beckoned me to sit with him on a curb in front of a gelato shop. Suddenly, he spoke to me in an excited voice: "Hai mai auuto una granita?" (Have you ever had granita?)

"No," I replied, "Che cos' e'?" (What is it?)

Into the shop he bounded and soon came out with a wonderful mixture of vanilla ice and lemon juice. "Questa e maravigliosa!" (This is marvelous!) I exclaimed.

We spoke together with extraordinary intensity about food, love, and life for an hour or so and then returned home keeping our conversation going. My host, Paolo, was amazed. "What happened?" he asked.

"Actually," I conjectured, "we've been talking to each other for a week—with our hearts."

Being open and sensitive doesn't necessitate spoken words. It does require an *empathic reach from the heart.* In fact, sometimes, it is better to be silent. Words are not always revealing, and, many times, people change their meaning into what they want to hear. Face-to-face, heart-to-heart communication bonds people together and pulls them from struggle because it rises out of the spirit that makes us all human.

Teach me to feel another's woe,
To hide the fault I see;
That mercy that I to others show,
That mercy show to me. (Alexander Pope)

Commitment 4: Make the Inside Connection (Centered Reflection)

People speak about hearing from God in and through nature, or through miraculous, revelatory acts, or as a voice literally from heaven above. When they distill these experiences down to the essential experience, however, we recognize they are speaking of what they have heard, actually, *from inside!* After all, since Copernicus told us our earth goes around the sun, not the reverse, we know that God is not literally above us listening for our pleas, our confessions, even our praise. God is, as our traditions teach us, omnipresent—*within* and among us—seeking union, hoping to bring to us new life, a new being, and new relationships—spiritual well-being.

How is this most vital connection made? Better, how is it hardwired, made constant? It's a particular challenge in today's helter-skelter world. Most people lead many lives: parents and parents to parents, a taxi service, short-order cooks, tutors, solvers of all manner of problems, nurturers, breadwinners, financial advisors, and suppliers of any number of things. For this reason, they struggle to discern what anchors their lives, what provides focus, what grants meaning beyond the immediate tasks, what they will look back on as significant in the last hours of their lives.[19]

Unfortunately, not only are there a myriad of distractions in life, but some people actually work to seal themselves off from their inner selves, even from connection with God. Nearly four out of ten of those we surveyed indicated that they were "sometimes afraid to listen to the voice within." I experienced this some years ago in dramatic fashion.

I was trapped in a tiny ski hut near the top of Mt. Baldy in Southern California, alone with my thoughts for more than forty-eight hours, with no means of contacting others (no cell phones or laptops then!). An unexpected snowstorm had shut off my escape—first out the front door (the only door!) and then to the trail to civilization. I kept warm and filled with the only edibles left—tea and popcorn. Every *National Geographic* and *Reader's Digest* was read and reread; the cabin was cleaned as never before; and sleep stole much of the remainder of my time.

My thoughts were dominated by mundane, sometimes silly, reflections. Was my car, far below in the parking area, facing north or south? Was the lot paved or crushed rock? In time, solitude forced me to become my own companion, an unusual position for me!

I found, to my surprise, that I wasn't ready to share much with my companion. I was about to make dramatic changes in my life, but I didn't use this rare opportunity to ponder these changes and their consequences. Upon reflection and with the objectivity the passage of time usually grants, I'm certain I was afraid to listen to my inner voice. I wasn't pleased with what it would say! Not long after, as time would prove, I made some very unwise decisions.[20]

This experience suggests that the voice inside—when heard—can reveal a clear and unadulterated message: I believe, God's message. It can tell us who we are and what we're about, and it can tell us where we should go. Perhaps this is why, so often, we keep it at bay through life chatter. To break in and connect, we have to become *centered*, disciplined, focused listeners. We have to develop a new attitude. Then, the connection can be completed. Usually, the proven pathways inside are prayer, meditation, or, powerfully, a combination—*centered reflection*: letting distractions go, quieting emotions (especially those blocking communication), getting attuned to our essential selves, going to the Source—for people of faith, God's spirit. When centered reflection becomes the first order of each day, it anchors life, clarifies who we are and who we can be. Those in our survey sample who describe themselves as spiritually strong agree with Question 6: "When I am open, God speaks to me."[21]

The ways of centered reflection (prayer, meditation, contemplation) are many, but one paramount result—feeling union with our inner self and with God—transcends all means. Centered reflection takes believers past *analyzing* messages, past *attempting to change* them, and certainly past *escaping* them, to *embracing* them. For this reason, centered reflection heals; it transforms; it inspires; most important, it positively affects our outlook, even amplifies left brain behavior. It transforms everyday living into inspired living, into the life the apostle Paul speaks of in his letter to the Colossians, "putting on love which is the bond of perfectness" (3:14).

Our research shows that the spiritual life and regular centered reflection go hand in hand. A life connected with

God keeps believers on the right path because all paths are illuminated and seen for where they lead. It grants confidence, worth, direction, wholeness, well-being. Disciplined, daily centered reflection brings a person's life picture into focus; *and it enables each to find, within, the Ultimate Friend.*[22]

Is this New Age theology, a departure from Christian traditions? On the contrary, it is at the heart of our traditions. This is not a call to extinguish the self or abandon faith; it is a call to discover one's authentic self and bond with the God who speaks to and through it within our faith tradition.

The spiritual life, in other words, does not come from obedience to external requirements of a foreign God outside the human frame, but from union with the God Within, in whose image we are made.

When people describe this journey of connection, they often speak of discovering, surprisingly and unexpectedly, a *child* within. Perhaps this is the meaning of Jesus' bold assertion that, unless we become as little children, we cannot enter the kingdom of heaven (Matt. 18:3).

As it turns out, we are never any particular age, birthdays and birth certificates aside. We always are children at heart. At sixteen years old, we are, so often, ten in judgment, thirty in our desires. But as we progress through life, society melds these ages and interests together into one age—maturity. So in adult lives, we are rewarded at home, on the job, even by close friends for "acting adult": for being responsible, task-oriented, prudent, controlled, sober. Maturity means we know what is expected and what risky behaviors to avoid. When things don't go smoothly or we are on the defensive, we ratchet up our maturity profile, becoming *robotically* "good"—at least for a while.

Maturity is the theme of most therapy sessions and sermons. People mend relationship breaches through supervised discussion, restrained words, and controlled actions (not through play—the way children resolve issues). Oftentimes, this tack leads into even more troubled waters and, ultimately, to greater struggle. Controlling speech and actions is like the experience

I have had reading from a teleprompter on television. Yes, my statements are concise and exact, but they also can be heard as forced and unnatural, even insincere, especially if someone else scripts them for me. Better in life to speak and act naturally, freely—surely playfully. It can be argued the family that plays together stays together. When people routinely and not so routinely engage in simple playfulness, when they expose the child within and bring that child into their relationships, they reconnect with their inner selves and overcome inauthenticity, even the threats of injustice, insecurity, and insincerity.

Discovering and engaging the child within—with a fine disregard for the rules of the game—is extraordinarily healing. It's a potent therapy. It relieves stress; it unveils options not possible in structured adult reality; and it expands our understanding and expression of self.[23] As Jesus counseled his disciples, "whoever receives a child in my name, receives me" (Luke 9:48).

There are many ways to release the playful nature. One sure way is to act like a child. Get down on the floor, roll around, sing fun songs, have inspirations, "smell the roses," preferably *with* little children. Act silly, tease dogs and adults, speak nonsense—even in loud tones. Hug in public, frolic in the snow, roll in piles of leaves, wear grubby clothes, let out pent-up feelings, and let in the fun of life. Acting like a child brings spontaneity back into life and lets out the guileless, constructive self within.

I frolic for these reasons and perhaps as a carryover from my Italian heritage or from my love of "extreme" challenges— skiing expert slopes (not as an expert), kayaking through giant ice floes on the perilous Grand River of Ohio in early springtime, surfing Hawaii's mammoth waves on a red flag day. Perhaps it comes from years of daily adventure with my son while he was growing up and my grandchildren today—nearly every day. But it also stems from paying heed to a mountain of research that shows that, while modern society has thrust its citizens progressively into a tightly molded regimen (the conformity of adulthood), fulfillment and contentment come most frequently from *breaking the mold*, living and relating spontaneously and joyfully, splicing childlike fun into every endeavor.[24]

> Peggy and Margaret, two college professors (can you think of any role more serious and straitlaced?) taught me early in my professional life how the child within us can bring relief to serious life and struggle, and energize others. Two very different women—one conservative, early forties, a perfect model of Talbot's finest; the other a staunch liberal, fifties, matronly in appearance. They team-taught U.S. history to crowded auditoriums of eager and enthusiastic students. Why their extraordinary appeal? (Students rarely clamor to take history.) It was their playfulness!
>
> They fanned the winds of gossip, featured the foibles and eccentricities of our nation's leaders, one and all, satirized each other's dearly held positions, engaged students in mock battles, ridiculed heroes, and strutted the classroom with provocation and abandon. They celebrated the child within them and drew out the child within their students: demystifying the obscure, liberating curiosity, turning ardor into play. And they held their students to the last seat in the back row and to the last day—captive! They taught me that even the most serious considerations can bring us joy when "adult" allows in "child."

Of course, we're not speaking of impulsive, out-of-control, anti-social behavior, but of open, good-natured spontaneity that builds and enhances caring relationships. It is paradoxical but, in uncanny ways, people can smile even in the face of great tragedy if they act out as a child.

It's never too late to have a happy childhood. It's never too late to make the inner connection. It is the threshold of spiritual well-being.

So, looking back over the commitments, *spiritual well-being moves from the inside out* and is expressed in caring, open relationships—in a word, in *love*. Seventy-two percent of our survey respondents agree. When they are moved from the inside, they are able to find peace and feel whole—spiritually and emotionally. The majority of those studied say this is the way God reveals himself to them[25] and grants to them a new life. As important, they believe they deserve the new life that comes from making the inside connection,[26] a life above destructive struggle. There is—and should be—no guilt here!

III

Living above "The Struggles"

*W*ith foundational connections secured, seekers are ready
to be carried forward by Scend to inspired living,
spiritual well-being.

A strange and revealing story is sandwiched into the book
of Genesis, just after Noah and the flood and immediately
before a recounting of Abraham's ancestry: the Tower of Babel
story (Gen. 11:1–9). *Strange,* because we find God inexplicably
alarmed that nomads wandering the desert plan to settle down
and build a tower that would reach into heaven. *Revealing,*
because the storyteller clearly believes these desert wanderers
could do such a thing. So likely were they to succeed that God
had to scramble their speech to interrupt their work. Apparently,
the author and early hearers of the story thought that God
resides above, perhaps on a canopy just a few hundred feet
above their settlements.

The story, of course ancient, provides a clue to how people
over millennia have visualized the spiritual landscape. God,

separate from humanity, is *above* in heaven—not too far away to prevent God from listening in and at times intervening, but far enough away to be superior to humanity, to be in command.

The message is: To find spiritual well-being, humans must send praise and pleas "heavenward" while being careful to be earthbound—obedient, humble, docile, tethered down here. The ambition, the striving that drove these settlers to challenge "heaven" must be supplanted by acquiescence to the constraining will of God. Then, and only then, will the connection with God be made.

Over the centuries since the Babel story's recounting, people have been sent on a myriad of spiritual migrations—from guru to guru, experience to experience—in search of the powerline to heaven, God's plan for the world, God's plan for their lives. These journeys usually have led to disappointment and heightened spiritual struggle. The faithful connect in special moments with the God beyond but—no matter how committed—soon disconnect because they are earthbound. They do God's will—then fall short of God's expectations.

Like the wildebeests of Africa's Serengeti Plain, these seekers are on *spiritual* migrations looking for sustenance and security, but they are never out of reach of predators. They hope for strength, but they become exhausted by the journey itself. They are certain security and justice come through judgment from above, that the God on high will reassure and secure, that they will find authentic living through a divinely imposed life agenda. With only a fragile link to the Almighty beyond, however, they fall short time and again—they struggle.

When we asked people to describe spiritual well-being, invariably they spoke of life "*above* destructive struggles," "a gold standard in living," "finding in *every waking moment* the power that affirms and grants purpose and meaning." They spoke of living through inspiration[1]—Scend. And when we asked the saints among us how that power is experienced in everyday life, they often talked in poetic terms: of smelling the sweet fragrance (Scent) of spiritual living, of inner delight balancing out their otherwise mundane lives. They related stories of exhilaration, hope, optimism, care, and strength.

I interviewed Iyanla Vanzant early in her publishing career. A few minutes into our discussion, I knew she wasn't another woman with a book. Hers was a story of Scend.

She was on her way by bus to pick up her welfare check when she read on an advertising panel over her seat: "Create a Better Future. Come to Medgar Evers College." She did.

"I'm out of here," she exclaimed, "out of welfare, on to college." How could she fashion such a turnaround in reality? She was, she revealed, compelled from inside to take a journey of faith. "It's in our blood, in our genes; we have designer genes," she exclaimed.

Her language—impassioned, intuitive, provocative. Her message: A-Scending.

Those who feel spiritually energized, like Iyanla, report consistently that they look *inside* to break the bonds of spiritual struggle. We conclude, therefore: Transformation occurs when connected people release a power within.

Commitment 5: Go Forward with Spirit (Inspiration)

One of the great enigmas of Christian history is *how* believers go about releasing the Spirit of Christ into their lives. Prayer has been the recommended methodology—personal and congregational. The assumption is that the God above releases the Spirit to those below—on request. So whatever the tradition, whether as pleas or recitations, prayers are offered with the hope the Receiver—external to the world—can and will listen in and respond. The language of prayer makes this clear. God is addressed as "above," "beyond," "on high," and, descriptively, with the power to intervene—"the Almighty,"

"Ruler of the Universe," "Creator," "Savior." Even when using the familial words "Father" and "Dear," prayers plead for the presence of the God transcendent.

Inspiration, however, is not understood—at least by our interviewees—as "called in" from the outside. It is seen as both divine *and* human in origin—for some, constantly there, always called up from the *inside*. The inspired are human but in a Christian way! Inspiration, in a word, is not mediated by prayer, even by the church; it is immediate.

Theological language and that of our research group participants reveal that people customarily believe spiritual well-being to be expressed in virtuous acts, transforming connections that come from the soul, by inspiration.

In fact, people from many cultures and almost all of the world's great religions (except Buddhism) speak of the nobility and resilience of the human spirit, of the dignity of the soul, and of hearing the inner voice of God's spirit. Perhaps this speech is mythical, not descriptive, but—especially in Western traditions—these words are understood to describe the core of emotions, the seat of enlightenment, the source of personal strength.[2] They speak of a power that people of all levels of sophistication—particularly, the saints among us—say they have witnessed, here called Scend: a surge from within that heals, resolves, *inspires*.

When our sample participants put detail to this experience, they talked about being open to the still, small, but awe-inspiring voice of God inside; of accepting and growing through the confusion of life; of embracing others—even strangers—through empathy and compassion; of connecting with their essential selves, the sacred, and with God. They spoke of healing breaches in relationships, of becoming one with others, of acting redemptively, not judgmentally. And they spoke of being empowered to live above struggle.

It is reasonable to conclude that spiritual power, life-changing energy, is always present, perhaps in the human community, certainly in believers. The shared human spirit—the spirit that has enabled many oppressed to endure, the victimized to demonstrate uncommon valor, unnotables to create remarkable beauty and advance the human condition—when elevated by God's spirit, *Scends* the faithful to live out their high calling.

Although women in our survey recognized the significance of Scend two to one over their male counterparts, most everyone identified with a "Yes" within, a power rising spontaneously from joining aspiration with inspiration, being vaulted forward as by a great wave, the Spirit of God. When the spirit that defines us as human connects with the divine Spirit, people are empowered. *Affirming the inner power and embracing the God Within* bring a new perspective on life and the spiritual well-being so commonly sought.

And the results? Focus group participants recount that when people embrace the God Within, they act virtuously—they do what is intrinsically good and they don't take away the opportunity of others to be good in the same way. They become the "salt of the earth." Their faith in Christ becomes activated in everyday living. As John Wesley is reported to have whispered as his dying words: "The best of all is this, that God is with us."

The world of peace and unity that modern peoples have clamored for through politics, commerce, and military might comes actually through putting these aside, accepting the vision of the Sermon on the Mount, the hope that love and Scend will cover us all and enable us to be peacemakers through God's grace and in the face of all threats.

The story of Dorothy in the Land of Oz comes to mind. She struggled to get back to her kinfolk in Kansas, traveling under great duress from Munchkinland to the Emerald City only to discover on the last page of her journey that her return to Kansas was within her power from her very first steps on the yellow brick road.

Dorothy in *The Wizard of Oz* learned—finally—from Glenda, the Good Witch: "You've always had the power to go home!"

As colorful, exciting, and anguishing as her dreamline to the Emerald City had been, as perplexing as her encounter with the wizard was, she already was back in Kansas—all she needed to do to escape her nightmare was Wake Up!

The saints among us describe their discovery of spiritual well-being in the same terms: finding what is resident within through Christ, tranScending struggle through healing transforming relationships, awakening to experience that lighthearted lilt we feel when we have won something big or gone to the beach on an early summer day—Scend.

When Christians reflect on this power, they commonly experience life as sacred, the connection with God hardwired through the redeeming work of Christ, the power to be Scent forward to break the hold of insecurity, to override cruel injustice and insincerity inherent in the human community, even among the "newborn." The Scend-inspired are those hardwired to self, to others, to the sacred, to God.

Struggles of spirituality transform into manageable challenges when Scend-filled relationships become primary, when people act from compassion and conscience, build from strengths and positive events, rediscover faith. When people feel and act from their inmost selves—their deeply embedded hopes and dreams—when they are inner-directed and propelled, they experience contentment, and they publicly and joyfully exult in their newfound state of spiritual well-being.

Liberation from fears of the world
Openness to our inmost selves
Expansion of our circle of comfort
The hope, the lilt of springtime
The color, the crisp of autumn
God with us in all seasons

IV

Sustaining a TranScendent Life

There are paragons of virtue, courage, and inspiration among us—average people and special people who live above spiritual struggle. They model for us spiritual well-being.

An acrid smell, then screams, filled the air. I was in the office of the president of the Borough of Manhattan Community College on a bright November day, looking out from seven stories up at a million tons of ugly rubble and a thousand firefighters protesting their removal from their fallen buddies. They no longer were needed, Mayor Giuliani directed. A confrontation between comrades—police and fire—was unfolding. It was 2001! Already traumatized office workers were certain a bloody riot was imminent. They couldn't hold back their fright, their anguish. They had witnessed enough mayhem. They had to call out in pain.

I met beautiful but fragile people that day. They had seen the horrific explosions, felt the earth shake, and then shake again; they had witnessed friends and strangers running in panic,

73

falling to their deaths from the World Trade Center towers. They had endured nearly two months of continuous, life-crushing disruptions—loss of phones and power and e-mail, and of lives. Their days were endless, their nights sleepless. Demands never placed before on leaders of any American college came at them in relentless waves. They were emotionally spent, physically fatigued, spiritually drained.

I had come to hear their stories, to understand their plight, and to fathom their resilience. The blows of the terrorists they still were enduring, but their spirits were undamaged: a painter who stayed on the job all night September 11 to help set up and run a triage center; the chief of public safety whose staff remained for days, though under siege, to keep the campus intact; a wonderful nurse who treated scores wounded mainly in soul; the public relations director who rose—and continued to rise—to a barrage of media, administrative, and student calls for explanation and assistance; the media director assigned to me with his student crew, shaken, weary, but so professional, so eager to serve; and a professor with healing in her heart, Dr. Susan Horowitz.

Fancy degrees from Chicago, Yale, and New York University aside, this professor of English warmed my heart, spoke to me—heart to heart—of courage, of resilience, of the nobility of the human spirit, and of trust, belief, empathy, centered reflection—overwhelmingly, of inspiration. She had a–Scended above the terrible struggles of the moment, struggles that had torn away her defenses and brought a pent-up world of hurts to the surface. "Don't mind my hair," she explained. "I'm not going to get it cut until my hairdresser starts back her salon. It's the least I can do for her."

I have met a number of saints: surely my mentor and teacher, Dr. Don Clifton (he has made this book valued and possible through his many kindnesses to me by inspiring me to his level of vision and research integrity, and by his warmth and care); and this petite but immensely strong educator, Susan.

Her stylist was still shut down, but her manicurist *had* come back to work. An immigrant from China working long hours—mostly in silence (she could speak little English)—she responded when Susan reached out "by impulse" to her. "Would you like a better life?" Susan gestured.

"I don't have time for classes," she conveyed in word and through awkward hand movements.

"Well, I'm going to teach you myself," Susan offered. "Do you like music? Then sing with me." Lesson One was under way: "You are my sunshine, my only sunshine. You make me happy when skies are gray..." As she related this story, we—together—broke out into singing: "You'll never know, Dear, how much I love you. Please don't take that sunshine away."

There were four Asian immigrant manicurists in the shop. Soon, every week, they sang together. Every week, they learned more English. Every week, they built trust, they believed, they felt Susan's remarkable empathy and compassion, they connected, they were inspired, they experienced the uplifting power of Scend.

The Scend-power I felt years ago when my mentor, the dean, reached out in Christian compassion to warm a lost and homeless soul, I witnessed this November day at Ground Zero.

Of course, one doesn't have to survive a terrorist attack to discover the power of Scend, to be spiritually energized. It requires—simply—connections: with one's primal self; with those who come into view, even for a few moments—the humble as well as the powerful; with what is sacred; certainly with the God who gives, sustains, and elevates lives. As the Jewish philosopher Martin Buber wrote a generation ago, "All real living is meeting."[1]

To have spiritual well-being is to be transformed—from insecurity, from inauthenticity, from being alone—to being cradled by the Spirit that binds us together and grants meaning, indeed high purpose, in life. Achieving spiritual well-being is moving from debilitating struggle to confident victory, from the rubble of life into the flowers of inspired living.

Susan occupies a pontifical seat of spiritual well-being. She, and thousands of other inspired rescuers and preservers, have taught us what is of lasting value and inherent virtue: human adaptation and resilience spiced with large doses of kindness, powered by Scend, the unquenchable fire of God's Spirit within. She teaches us that we must make—in thought and action—a paradigm shift: from searching for salvation from the God beyond to living redemptively through the God Within.

Of course, life—even powered by Scend—isn't a continuous whoosh. Struggles are an inescapable part of life. Waves glide us beachward but, to take the next, we have to go up against strong currents. The difference is that struggle to gain new release builds affirmation; struggle to keep one's head above water debilitates.

I'm always struck by the excitement and propulsion that first-of-their-family college students exhibit when they come to know that they, too, can succeed—even in competition with the children of the elite! That same energized empowerment is present with those who come to experience the power of spiritual living—who celebrate this new reality, overcoming life struggles in the twenty-first century.

Now, as they say to newlyweds in Italy:

Avanti con Effusione—Go forward with passion and
  Spirit!

A Scend above the Struggles

APPENDIX A

The Research Base

The responses to surveys of 486 adult Americans[1] selected to mirror anticipated readers (those in search of spiritual well-being) undergird this book. Some in the sample already are models of spiritual strength. Their responses were separated out and scrutinized to determine common traits and commitments. The instrument used is the Index of Spirituality developed by the author in consultation with Dr. Donald Clifton, longtime chair and CEO of The Gallup Organization (see Appendix B).[2] Index questions were derived from comments of more than twelve hundred participants in seventy-six focus groups who related real-life stories about spiritual struggles and victories over them. Focus group participants identified what was holding them back (their struggles), then they ranked these struggles in order of life importance. Finally, they talked through strategies they have found effective in overcoming spiritual struggle or have witnessed in others. Those who spoke of and exhibited what we call Scend in their lives were sorted out from the others so the ingredients of the Scend experience could be identified and clarified. The Five Commitments described in the book, however, derive from survey analysis. These commitments correlate with perceived individual spirituality. When they are expressed in the life of a family, a business, a school, a congregation, they likely will multiply in effect and form a beacon of positive energy and goodness where people thrive personally and collectively and communities are transformed.

The extensive professional literature on happiness, flow, and life satisfaction was reviewed carefully—from Seligman to Kahneman to Diener to Emmons to Csikszentmihalyi (cited in footnotes to the text) and a number of others along the way. These "positive psychologists" were helpful. They have linked spirituality to subjective well-being;[3] but they have not set forth how the formidable challenges to spiritual well-being (the struggles) can be overcome.

Our pathway to spiritual well-being includes perspectives from philosophy, psychology, and Eastern traditions. This does not represent an abandonment of the Christian faith. Christian thought accepted, early on, the conceptual framework of Greek philosophy and was enhanced, not undermined, by it.[4] We can grow—and we should—from all spiritually constructive approaches.

APPENDIX B

Index of Spirituality Survey

The Index of Spirituality Survey (pp. 80–85) was developed by James Catanzaro in consultation with Dr. Donald Clifton of The Gallup Organization.

Index of Spirituality

Please rate each of the following statements on a scale of 1 to 5, where 1 is strongly disagree, 2 is disagree, 3 is neither agree nor disagree, 4 is agree, and 5 is strongly agree.

	Strongly Disagree			Strongly Agree		Does Not Apply /NA
1. I like to be alone to think.	1	2	3	4	5	6
2. In the last week, I have prayed or meditated at least 20 minutes each day.	1	2	3	4	5	6
3. When I pray or meditate, I discover who I really am.	1	2	3	4	5	6
4. I take time daily to connect with God's purpose for my life.	1	2	3	4	5	6
5. There is more to life than I have experienced.	1	2	3	4	5	6
6. When I am open, God speaks to me.	1	2	3	4	5	6
7. I am filled with the Holy Spirit.	1	2	3	4	5	6
8. My belief in God makes me feel secure.	1	2	3	4	5	6
9. My belief in God takes me above life's struggles.	1	2	3	4	5	6

	1	2	3	4	5	6
10. I listen to the voice within me.	1	2	3	4	5	6
11. When I listen with my heart, I can actually feel what the other person feels.	1	2	3	4	5	6
12. I feel the pain that others feel.	1	2	3	4	5	6
13. I respond to the pain that others feel.	1	2	3	4	5	6
14. Self-reflection and prayer are ways I get in touch with myself.	1	2	3	4	5	6
15. I sense the power others have for doing good.	1	2	3	4	5	6
16. I feel the love of other people.	1	2	3	4	5	6
17. When I listen, God speaks to me.	1	2	3	4	5	6
18. I have cared for another person for at least 10 years.	1	2	3	4	5	6
19. There is a person who has cared for me for at least 10 years.	1	2	3	4	5	6
20. For one million dollars, I would be tempted to give up my relationship with my closest friend.	1	2	3	4	5	6
21. There are people in my life that I will love, whatever they did.	1	2	3	4	5	6

	1	2	3	4	5	6
22. I have never met a person I could not love.	1	2	3	4	5	6
23. When I feel loved, I feel I can overcome any obstacle.	1	2	3	4	5	6
24. My finest expression is to love someone who needs me.	1	2	3	4	5	6
25. Sometimes, I am afraid to listen to my inner voice.	1	2	3	4	5	6
26. Sometimes, I have conversations with my inner self.	1	2	3	4	5	6
27. My spiritual well-being always comes from within.	1	2	3	4	5	6
28. Messages and demands from the outside require so much of my attention that I have little or no time for reflection.	1	2	3	4	5	6
29. I worry because I have so many things I cannot do very well.	1	2	3	4	5	6
30. I feel I must overcome my weaknesses before I can be strong.	1	2	3	4	5	6
31. I am completely satisfied with my spiritual life.	1	2	3	4	5	6
32. I believe I have a soul, a spiritual dimension.	1	2	3	4	5	6
33. Sometimes, I act like a child, and I enjoy it very much.	1	2	3	4	5	6

	1	2	3	4	5	6
34. Within the last month, I voluntarily helped a person in crisis.	1	2	3	4	5	6
35. I am close to the people with whom I work.	1	2	3	4	5	6
36. I am a hugger.	1	2	3	4	5	6
37. I know the warmth that comes when I really understand the feelings of others.	1	2	3	4	5	6
38. Others trust me to keep their secrets.	1	2	3	4	5	6
39. I seem to have an uncanny sense for making other people feel good.	1	2	3	4	5	6
40. I have been hurt by someone close to me in the past.	1	2	3	4	5	6
41. I enter into new relationships readily even though I have had disappointments.	1	2	3	4	5	6
42. I am loyal to my partner in life.	1	2	3	4	5	6
43. I would have an intimate relationship outside marriage if my lover was disloyal.	1	2	3	4	5	6
44. I am consistently faithful to my basic values and ideals at work.	1	2	3	4	5	6
45. My life is hurried and complicated.	1	2	3	4	5	6
46. I know where I want to go in life and I'm heading there.	1	2	3	4	5	6

	1	2	3	4	5	6
47. I know what my basic values are and they guide me in my everyday life.	1	2	3	4	5	6
48. I seek people who are inspiring.	1	2	3	4	5	6
49. I've known people who appear to be carried forward by a positive power within them.	1	2	3	4	5	6
50. Sometimes, I feel I'm carried forward as if by a great wave.	1	2	3	4	5	6

Following are some demographic questions to be used for research purposes.

Date you completed the survey: _____   What is your gender? _____ Male   _____ Female

What is your education level?

_____ Less than high school graduate   _____ Trade/technical/vocational training

_____ High school graduate   _____ College graduate

_____ Some college   _____ Postgraduate work/degree

What is your age?

_____ Under 18   _____ 25–30   _____ 37–42   _____ 49–54

_____ 18–24   _____ 31–36   _____ 43–48   _____ 55–60   _____ 61+

What is your religious preference?

_____ Jewish	_____ Methodist
_____ Mormon	_____ Greek Orthodox
_____ Nazarene	_____ Religious Science
_____ Roman Catholic	_____ Holiness
_____ Christian	_____ Church of God
_____ Nondenominational	_____ Buddhist
_____ Jehovah's Witness	_____ Episcopalian
_____ Pentecostal	_____ Presbyterian
_____ Church of Christ	_____ Baptist
_____ Atheist/Humanist	_____ Latter Day Saints
_____ Unitarian	_____ Christian Science
_____ Hindu	_____ Lutheran
_____ Assembly of God	_____ Seventh Day Adventist
_____ Muslim	_____ Other Protestant
_____ Apostolic	

APPENDIX C

Summary: Index of Spirituality Respondents

Two batches of Index responses were analyzed. Batch 1 was drawn in Spring 2001 from college students in religion classes and adults at places of worship in California, Illinois, and Tennessee; Batch 2 was drawn in Fall 2001 from students and parishioners in Massachusetts, New York, Texas, Tennessee, Florida, and Alabama. Among all of the respondents, 44.2 percent were ages 17 to 32 years; 32.5 percent ages 33 to 48; and 23.3 percent ages 49 and older. Sixty-eight percent were women; 96 percent were Caucasian. Also, 61.6 percent were Protestants of all denominations, 22.2 percent Roman Catholics, and 12.1 Episcopalians. Jews, Muslims, Orthodox Christians, Hindus, Buddhists, and atheists were represented in the sample but each number less than five. There were no significant discontinuities between Batch 1 and Batch 2 despite regional differences and a stronger representation of Roman Catholics in Batch 2.

Women reported higher in all measures of spiritual strength, significantly so in trust, empathy, and Scend. Most measures show Catholics and Protestants to be very close in strength of spiritual indicators except belief (faith; see chapter 2, note 8). Jews, Hindus, Buddhists, Muslims, humanists, and others were so small in sample size as to make comparisons unreliable.

Age and education (more than 90 percent of the sample had at least some college study) revealed no significant variances in reporting.

APPENDIX D

Focus Group Research

It took more than forty focus groups centered on life struggles—of college students, church members, and conference attendees—to realize that spiritual well-being was key to the understanding of all life struggles, whatever one's age, gender, race, socioeconomic level, or religious preference.

Once I recognized that the ultimate struggles were with connections—with oneself, important others, what we believe to be sacred, and with God, then subsequent focus groups could zero in on issues of life purpose, security, authenticity, and transforming connections: spirituality.

The thirty-three focus groups that have been conducted since that recognition involved more than 550 participants. (More than 1,200 were engaged in all.) Twenty-seven were conducted between 1999 and 2001 of college students through introductory classes (so as to ensure a wide and varied population), five were at churches (Sunday school classes), and one at a conference of professional educators.

Responses to all questionnaires and group discussions were analyzed to determine continuities: pervasive life struggles, how they are described, and successful strategies in overcoming them. Of particular importance was to learn when challenges turn from being stimulants for heightened performance to destructive enemies of subjective well-being, and how inspiration grants the resilience to live above damaging struggles.

The continuities identified have become the basis of the book's discussion of struggles and the description of Scend. They also provided the basis for the fifty-question Index of Spirituality.

Demographics were not kept for all sessions, but we can estimate—based on related data—that 61 percent were women, 17 percent African American, three percent Hispanic, and two percent Asian. Also, 28.6 percent were ages 17 to 21 years, 43.8 percent were 22 to 34, 22.2 percent were 35 to 64, and 5.4 percent were 65 and older. Breakdown by religious preference is not available.

Two "struggles" questionnaires were developed and used. In the first ten groups, participants were asked to think about their own situations in terms of forty life struggles and rate 1 to 10 (where 1 is no struggle and 10 a great struggle) challenges to well-being and life success. These were narrowed for subsequent groups to the seven most highly rated: relationships, stress, finances, time management, motivation, health, and spirituality. The participants in seven focus groups were asked to complete, as well, the Fordyce Emotions Questionnaire to determine subjective well-being (happiness quotient) and to compare findings with questionnaire results.

APPENDIX E

Five Commitments: Spiritual Well-Being Data

These contributors to spiritual well-being occur with the following reliability according to data from 343 respondents to the Index of Spirituality Survey:

Two Measurements of Component Strength		
Trust	1.4569	.75
Belief	1.8822	.80
Empathy	1.6121	.82
Connecting	1.5843	.91
Scend	1.5632	.73
	(on a scale of 1=minimum significance to 2=maximum)	

See charts on the following pages for distribution. The horizontal axis of each chart corresponds to the options of response in the survey (1=strongly diagree; 5=strongly agree). The vertical axis shows the number of respondents.

TRUST

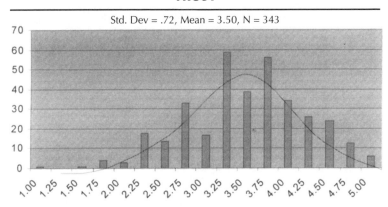

BELIEF

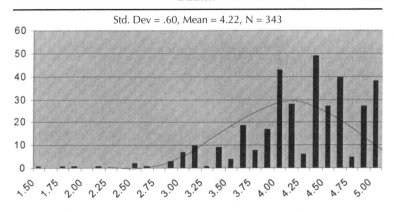

EMPATHY

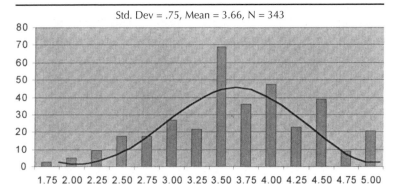

CONNECTING

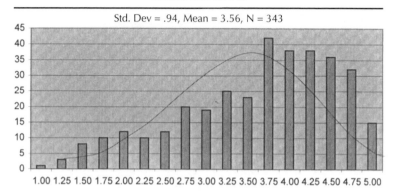

Std. Dev = .94, Mean = 3.56, N = 343

SCEND

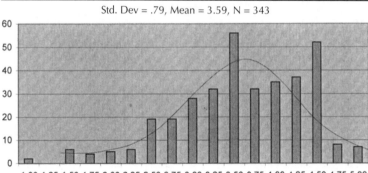

Std. Dev = .79, Mean = 3.59, N = 343

Schema of the Book

Spiritual Surfing

The Preparation
Four Planted Steps
to Get into Position

Reorienting
Our Lives

The Glide
One Streamlined
Commitment to Live
Powered by Scend

Transforming
Our Lives

Spiritual Struggles/
Disconnections

The Vulnerable Life

Newfound
Spiritual
Well-being/
Vital Connections

Connected,
Scend-filled Living

Life above the
Struggles

Notes

Introduction

[1]"Spirituality" leads to purpose, unity, and transcendence. Its specific expression differs from tradition to tradition, individual to individual. Our survey sample showed that those who connect regularly and intuitively agree disproportionately with Question 31: "I am completely satisfied with my spiritual life."

[2]Derived from those defining experiences that make up our life's narrative as well as from gene expression.

[3]The reality of God traditionally is seen as independent of our religious experience. See John B. Cobb, Jr., *God and the World* (Philadelphia: Westminster Press, 1969), 126.

[4]Eighty-three percent of those surveyed indicated they had "known people who appear to be carried forward by a positive power within them," but only 22 percent agree strongly that they themselves have had such an experience.

[5]Analysis of our Index of Spirituality results shows struggle (stress) correlates negatively with experiencing spiritual well-being (belief, reflection, trust, inspiration).

[6]Norman Bradburn discovered that positive and negative affect are not on a continuum: Norman M. Bradburn, *Structure of Psychological Well-Being* (New York: National Opinion Research Center, 1969). Overcoming negative affect doesn't deliver, automatically, positive affect. That must be achieved directly. So, I believe, while spiritual well-being is undercut by struggle, it cannot be achieved only through struggle reduction. Direct efforts are required to build and sustain transforming connections.

[7]See Ed Diener and Eunkook Mark Suh, "National Differences in Subjective Well-Being," in *Well-Being: The Foundations of Hedonic Psychology* (New York: Russell Sage Foundation, 1999), 434ff. The Gallup Organization surveys uncovered similar findings as early as 1976.

[8]In our research, seventy-six focus groups (that engaged more than 1,200 randomly selected individuals in the United States and England over five years) revealed no significant difference in reporting life struggles between those who self-assessed as happy and unhappy.

[9]Ed Diener reported to Positive Psychology Summit 2000 participants that he gives a B+ to the correlation and causal relationship between happiness and sociability and between happiness and health, and a B to that between happiness and success and between happiness and longevity (Washington, D.C., October 15, 2000).

[10]See "The Health of the Nation," a report from The Gallup Organization, November 1998, 14 and 62. One of every two adults experiences at least one "bad" mental health day monthly and one in ten, ten or more days monthly; one in ten reports that they have seriously considered suicide. Only 15 percent of our survey respondents disagreed with the statement, "Life is hurried and complicated."

[11]These qualities capture what is common to the differing descriptions of the following traditions: Eastern Orthodox, devotional community life; Roman Catholic, sacramental community life; Evangelical Protestant, godly individual living; Liberal Protestant, socially concerned living; New Age, authentic individual living; Buddhist, awakened living; Hindu, tolerant living from duty; Muslim, submissive living; Jewish, sanctified living.

[12]There is no better demonstration than African American practices of Christianity. Holding to the same scriptures, doctrines, and creeds as the dominant culture, Blacks in America worship in ways shaped by their journey from the imponderables of slavery through the turbulent streets of the 1960s and 1970s to the unfinished business of social equity today. Connecting with the ancient children of Israel in their struggle with oppressing powers, and with Jesus who was persecuted through no fault of his own, Blacks interpret scripture and worship in ways so different that all the forces of integration have not moved them to White congregations; nor have Whites, especially liberal Whites who have courageously supported the civil rights movement, moved to Black churches.

[13]Paul Tillich, *The Courage To Be* (New Haven: Yale University Press, 1947), 37. See also Tillich, *Systematic Theology*, Vol. 1 (Chicago: University of Chicago Press, 1951), 248–49.

¹⁴Aristotle, "Nicomachean Ethics," in *The Works of Aristotle* vol. 2 of Great Books of the Western World (Chicago: Encyclopaedia Britannica, Inc., 1952), 340.

¹⁵This merging of spiritual well-being into a description of happiness is new in the West. For the better part of two millennia, the pursuit of the good life was traceable to the ancient Greeks, while a quite different interest, the pursuit of righteousness, had its origins in the Judeo-Christian ethic. In this postmodern era—and certainly here in this work—it is assumed that righteousness leads to happiness, that the two traditions, therefore, can be brought together amicably and meaningfully. Of course, there has been a longstanding belief that morality and true happiness go hand in hand, and it is indisputable that many early cultures associated morality with the divine. The Babylonian sun god Shamash gives a code of laws to King Hammurabi, and the God of the Old Testament grants to Moses the Ten Commandments.

¹⁶Just as great Renaissance painters (the Florentine artists whose works adorn the Uffizi Gallery) portrayed Jesus, Mary, and the disciples—even God the Father—with human warmth and expression, so our figure is inspired but every bit human.

¹⁷Optimism is a recent outlook of Western peoples. Samuel Johnson, in 1755, didn't even include the word in his first dictionary, and though Helen Keller wrote a famous essay on the subject as a young adult at the turn of the past century, she was quick to concede in her mature writings that she had lacked insight into human nature when she spoke optimistically of the possibilities of humanity. See Joseph P. Lash, *Helen and Teacher: The Story of Helen Keller and Anne Sullivan Macy* (New York: Delacorte Press, 1980), 307–308.

¹⁸Marcus Buckingham and Donald O. Clifton, *Now, Discover Your Strengths* (New York: Free Press, 2001).

¹⁹Scend, as derived from *Webster's New World Dictionary of the American Language,* edited by David B. Guralnik, 2d college ed. (Cleveland: W. Collins, 1980): The surge upward and forward under the influence of a powerful natural force, as on a wave.

²⁰See S. Smith and P. Razzell, *The Pools Winners* (London: Caliban Books, 1975); also, P. Brickman, D. Coates, and R. Janoff-Bulman, "Lottery Winners and Accident Victims: Is Happiness Relative?" *Journal of Personality and Social Psychology* 36 (August 1978): 917–27.

²¹Middle-class Americans (with family incomes of circa $50,000 a year) registered in 2000 virtually the same satisfaction with life as those making $90,000. While income has grown markedly from the 1950s to the present, no improvement in self-reported subjective well-being has occurred (Hazel Markus, "Culture and the Good Life," Positive Psychology Summit 2001, Washington, D.C., October 7, 2001).

²²Religiosity is widespread throughout the world, but studies of separated identical twins reveal that it varies significantly in the human community based on inheritance. See Martin E. P. Seligman, *What You Can Change and What You Can't* (New York: Fawcett Columbine, 1993), 43.

²³"Self" is that which integrates the various components of the psyche; it develops as we piece together throughout life a narrative that ties together our past and present experience of our selves. See Brian L. Lancaster, "On the Relationship between Cognitive Models and Spiritual Maps," *Journal of Consciousness Studies* 7, no. 11–12 (2000): 236.

Chapter 1: Understanding "The Struggles"

¹"The percentage of Americans who say they feel the need in their lives to experience spiritual growth surged twenty-four points in just four years—from 58 percent in 1994 to 82 percent in 1998." George Gallup, Jr., and D. Michael Lindsay, *Surveying the Religious Landscape* (Harrisburg: Morehouse Publishing, 1999), 1.

²Seligman, *What You Can Change*, 246–47.

³There is abundant data to show that faith is important to healing, but the data indicate that *any* faith can provide the encouragement needed for faster recovery. In other words, giving assent to a specific doctrine doesn't correlate with gains in coping with disease or with healing, but giving assent in general does. See Dale A. Matthews, *The Faith Factor* (New York: Penguin Books, 1992), passim.

⁴If God did intervene on behalf of the righteous, insurance companies and those who wager on sports would be beating a path to them!

[5]An obvious case is the believer who seeks guidance for family building from the New Testament but finds exhortations to push free of family to follow the cross.

[6]Those sampled with the highest indication of struggle agreed or strongly agreed disproportionately with Question 30: "I feel I must overcome my weaknesses before I can be strong."

[7]Lawrence Ferlinghetti, *A Coney Island of the Mind* (New York: New Directions Publishing, 1958), 88.

[8]See S. Jay Olshansky, Bruce A. Carnes, and Robert N. Butler, "If Humans Were Built to Last," *Scientific American* 284 (March 2001): 51.

[9]James Baldwin, "Notes of a Native Son" in *Voices in Our Blood: America's Best on the Civil Rights Movement*, ed. by Jon Meacham (New York: Random House, 2001), 367.

Chapter 2: Breaking from "The Struggles"

[1]Yes, optimism can cause us to misjudge the severity of threats, to see real-life situations through rose-colored (instead of clear) glasses. But, on the other hand, our abilities to adapt and cope are enhanced greatly by an optimistic outlook—and these abilities track well with feeling happy. See Lauren B. Alloy, Lyn Y. Abramson, and Alexandra M. Chiara, "On the Mechanisms by which Optimism Promotes Positive Mental and Physical Health: A Commentary on Aspinwall and Brunhart," in *The Science of Optimism and Hope*, ed. by Jane E. Gillham (Philadelphia: Templeton Foundation Press, 2000), 201–8.

[2]In our research, exhibiting trust and loyalty is correlated strongly with being Scent—feeling one is "carried forward as if by a great wave"—and satisfied with one's spiritual life.

[3]Shepherd of Hermas II.27. "Visions," The Shepherd of Hermas, Roberts-Donaldson Translation, in *The Ante-Nicene Fathers: Translations of the Writings of the Fathers down to A.D. 325*, vol. 2, edited by Alexander Roberts and James Donaldson, et al. (Peabody, Massachusetts: Hendrickson Pubishers, Inc., 1994). God is angry with Hermas because he violated his marriage through evil desires and did not warn his sons of corruptions. When Hermas and his sons repent, they are enrolled in the Book of Life as saints. A righteous man pleases God through a righteous family. See chapters 1 and 3.

[4]Roy F. Baumeister, Ellen Bratslavsky, Catrina Finkenauer, and Kathleen D. Vohs, *Bad Is Stronger Than Good*, forthcoming.

[5]For a complete account of these tales, see Richard Chase, *The Jack Tales* (Boston: Houghton Mifflin, 1943).

[6]Andrew Newberg and Eugene D'Aquili, *Why God Won't Go Away: Brain Science and the Biology of Belief* (New York: Ballantine Books, 2001), 129. The mystical experience appears to have been formative to the world's major religions—found in large doses in Hinduism, Buddhism, and Taoism, as well as a well-recognized stream (though sometimes subterranean and oftentimes disturbing) of Judaism, Christianity, and Islam. The need to purge oneself of the contamination of the world and suspend one's faculties, though common, is not understood here. What is understood is union with self and the Transcendent as transforming. This experience takes form in Christianity based on Jesus' vision described in the gospel of John. It is of his spiritual union with followers after his return (see chapters 14—17). The Pauline epistles are influential, as well. They are laced with references to the apostle's desire to be one—personally and profoundly—with Christ. Though always ennobling, Christian mystical experience is not necessarily ecstatic or revelatory. It simply discerns the "Beyond" that is "Within."

[7]Augustine, *The Confessions*, vol. 18 of Great Books of the Western World (Chicago: Encyclopedia Brittanica, 1952).

[8]In the Greek of the New Testament, "belief," "believe," and "faith" all come from a single root word, *pisteuo*. Belief and faith are one.

[9]Roman Catholics, by percentage, reported significantly less agreement with belief/faith statements in the Index of Spirituality than Protestants—likely because of the high-definition Roman Catholic emphasis on church authority and dogma (61.6 percent for Protestants, 36.6 percent for Roman Catholics).

[10]Gallup and Lindsay, *Surveying the Religious Landscape.*

[11]Those in the sample who are spiritually connected agreed disproportionately with Question 47: "I know what my basic values are, and they guide me in my everyday life."

[12]Mihaly Csikszentmihalyi, *Finding Flow: The Psychology of Engagement with Everyday Life* (New York: Basic Books, 1998).

[13]See Diana L. Eck, *A New Religious America* (San Francisco: HarperSanFrancisco, 2001), 66–67.

[14]Respondents to the Index of Spirituality associate empathy with spiritual well-being (a correlation of 4.2 occurs between affirming responses to belief, inspiration, and empathy questions).

[15]Donald O. Clifton and Paula Nelson, *Soar with Your Strengths* (New York: Dell Publishing, 1992), 147.

[16]The Gallup StrengthsFinder studies show some people exhibit high levels of empathy as personal traits, consistent near-perfect performance in an activity, in this case, consistently "feeling the emotions of those around you...(as) your own." (See Buckingham and Clifton, *Now, Discover Your Strengths,* 25 and 97.) Others do not. We can conclude, therefore, that we must either develop empathy as our inherent strength or learn how to express it when it isn't one of our dominant traits, like actors mimic behavior.

[17]When we recognize superordinate values—those that transcend groups and tie us all together—we can treat others fairly, as members of *our* group. When larger group identity isn't cultivated, we tend to treat others instrumentally.

[18]Robert Nozick argues that it is the loss of both parents that makes our own mortality real to us. "We're next in line—no one is supposed to die first." See Robert Nozick, *The Examined Life* (New York: Simon & Schuster, 1998), 20.

[19]This is why there is a significant correlation between being religious and reporting satisfaction with life. There is a clear and salutary effect from having a sense of meaning and purpose. See Michael Argyle, "Causes and Correlates of Happiness," in *Well-Being: The Foundations of Hedonic Psychology,* ed. by Daniel Kahneman, Ed Diener, and Norbert Schwarz (New York: Russell Sage Foundation, 1999), 365.

[20]Curiously, women report they are more likely to be afraid (sometimes) "to listen to my inner voice" than men (3.20 mean versus a 2.81 mean on a 5-point scale).

[21]Almost two-thirds of our sample's respondents report that connections with both the self and God are made through focused prayer (or meditation). Nevertheless, only one in four says such prayer is an important dimension in his life.

[22]Dr. Nell Mohney, "Mentoring with Vivacious Calm," *Chattanooga on the Move* (Summer 2001): 7.

[23]Charles Schaefer study cited in "Play Therapy," *Industry Week* 245, no. 15 (19 August 1996).

[24]Ibid.

[25]George Gallup, Jr., *Religion in America: 1996* (Princeton: The Princeton Religion Research Center, 1996), 24.

[26]When we believe we deserve well-being, we covet it and our sense of well-being is enhanced further; also, our commitments are strengthened. See E. Tory Higgins, *Handbook of Motivation and Cognition: Foundations of Social Behavior,* vol. 2 (New York: Guilford Press, 1998), passim.

Chapter 3: Living above "The Struggles"

[1]The inspired in our sample agreed strongly with Question 10: "I listen to the voice within me."

[2]Thales, the first philosopher, spoke of the soul as the center of emotions, knowledge, even locomotion. The notion is Greek in origin and ancient, but it is behind our contemporary experience, as well—personal and religious.

Chapter 4: Sustaining a TranScendent Life

[1]Martin Buber, *I and Thou* (New York: Charles Scribner's Sons, 1970), 55.

Appendix A: The Research Base

[1] A purposive sample of 486 Americans (designed to replicate the likely reader audience consisting of those who say they are on a journey to find spiritual well-being) was surveyed in 2001 to determine levels of spiritual satisfaction and the nature of spiritual struggle. The 486 consisted of two drawn samples: 138 from California, Tennessee, and Illinois; and 348 from Massachusetts, Texas, New York, Florida, and Alabama. Fifty questions, drawn from seventy-six focus groups, were asked the Index of Spirituality (see Appendix B) to determine correlations with spiritual satisfaction and the nature and extent of struggle. Responses were analyzed to determine factors (underlying connectivities), correlations—positive and negative—and to establish reliability coefficients among the factors. Education, age, region of the country, gender, and religious affiliation (preference) were examined to determine possible reporting variances. Few significant variances were found. Five continuities, however, emerged. They became the spine of the book: trust, belief, empathy, connection, and Scend. See Appendix C for detail on the sample and findings.

[2] The Index of Spirituality codesigned by Dr. Don Clifton of The Gallup Organization and the author was distributed nationwide to 486 respondents and factor analyzed (see Apprendix E).

[3] Robert A. Emmons and Chi Cheung, "Assessing Spirituality through Personal Goals: Implications for Research on Religion and Subjective Well-Being," *Social Indicators Research* 45 (November 1998): 415.

[4] This argument is made persuasively by John Cobb, Jr., in *Christ in a Pluralistic Age* (Philadelphia: Westminster Press, 1975), 204–5.

Index

Mellencamp, John Cougar, 6

Native Americans, 56–57

playfulness, 63–65
Pope, Alexander, 60
Price, Vincent, 54–55

Scend
  definition, 8, 9
  experience of, 68–69, 72,
  75
  how to promote, 10, 12
Schleifstein, Mark, 46
September 11, 2001, 4–5, 15,
  20, 22, 40, 50, 51, 53, 73–
  74
spirit (divine), 10, 11, 13, 45,
  46, 62, 69–72, 75–76
spirit (human), 2, 9, 31–32,
  70–71
spirituality
  definition, 1, 3
  and religiosity, 18–19
  and "truth," 41–49
  and well-being, 5–6, 8, 19
streamlining, spiritual, 44–45
"Struggles, The" (*see also,*
  Contents)
  definition, xii
  descriptions, 4–7
  with inauthenticity, 27–29
  with injustice, 23–25
  with insecurity, 20–22
  with insincerity, 25–27
surfing, spiritual analogy to,
  vii–viii, 8, 10–11, 13, 92

Teller, Edward, 31–32
Tower of Babel (Gen. 11:1–9),
  67–68
trust, 32–41

Vanzant, Iyanla, 69

Wesley, John, 71
Wizard of Oz, 71–72